BEYOND THE

A Time Of Awakening

SAZMICK BOOKS

Beyond The Illusion – A Time Of Awakening

First published February 2011 by Sazmick Books

Email: walkintothelight@live.co.uk

Web: http://www.walkintothelight.co.uk
Web: http://www.earthshinesanctuary.com

© Michael & Sarah Feeley. All rights reserved

No part of this book may be reproduced, stored in a retrieval system, or transmitted by any means without the written permission of the authors.

British Library Cataloguing-in Publication Data
A catalogue record for this book is available from the British Library

ISBN: 978-0-9556103-1-7

Printed and bound in the UK

SAZMICK BOOKS

BEYOND THE ILLUSION

A Time Of Awakening

Michael & Sarah Feeley

Also available from Michael & Sarah Feeley

From Ghosts and Poltergeist activity... to UFO's and Out of Body Experiences... to Angels, Energy and Meditation and much more!

In the early hours of one February morning in 2009 something happened to Michael & Sarah that was to change their lives forever. A terrifying and dramatic awakening occurred which set them on their path of enlightenment.

Now they experience amazing phenomena including celestial visitation, UFO sightings and communication, Astral Projection and much more. From childhood experiences to the current day, this book connects many of the dots between 'unexplainable' phenomena and will have you glued from cover to cover...

This book will change the way you see Life (and death) forever...

ISBN: 978-0- 956610-300

Available from: www.walkintothelight.co.uk | Amazon.co.uk | Many Waterstones stores throughout the UK

Artwork by Sarah Feeley

Some of Sarah's artwork can be seen in this book. It often depicts the awakening of humanity and inspires people to raise their own vibrations and to reconnect with their soul and the higher realms of consciousness.

Sarah also paints personal custom Angelic portraits of humans and animals, an ideal gift for friends and family.

More examples can be found on Michael & Sarah's website:

www.walkintothelight.co.uk

ACKNOWLEDGEMENTS

Our thanks and appreciation goes out to the following:

Our family, immediate and extended, you are very dear to us.

Karen D, for your inspiration and advice and of course your loyal friendship.

Lynda B, for your energetic assistance and perseverance during times of opposition to our work.

Geoff B, for your gentle persuasion on those cold evenings in the park, without which, we would have stayed at home in the warm! Also for allowing the use of some of your pictures in this book.

To all of our friends, past and present.

To the Angelic, Cosmic and Spirit realms for your guidance and your continued support.

Planet Earth for your patience.

Bonnie, welcome to the family.

And also dedicated to the loving memory of all those who we knew and loved as physical beings, pets and human, who are now at a different level of consciousness and awareness in another place; you are missed. We'll see you all again at some point in the future...

In Love Always...

Michael & Sarah

CONTENTS

ABOUT THE AUTHORS

Michael and Sarah Feeley met in late 2005 when they worked together as frontline police officers in the United Kingdom. After a few years together they married and now enjoy life as Husband and Wife.

In 2009 their life was to change forever and it changed in traumatic circumstances when they both relived the murder of a 14 year old Victorian teenager at the same time, but seemingly on another dimension. This was to alter their life's path forever and for Michael and Sarah, reality would never be the same ever again.

This event gave them both a spiritual wake up call and an awakening that they couldn't sleep through, and soon after, the twin flame team left their careers in the police force to spread their light. They began to interact with and see Angels, UFO's, Ascended Masters, Spirit guides,

Guardian Angels, and relatives that had left the physical realm and had returned to speak with them. Information began to fall at their feet and it was obvious to them that this was building them up to something very special. They soon realised that they were on a mission of great importance.

Michael and Sarah documented their amazing experiences and the start of their spiritual journey of awakening in their first book *Walk Into The Light - The Journey Of A Lightworker Duo* which has proven to be very popular having changed many of its reader's outlooks on life and in some cases, their lives altogether. The message of the book was one of beauty and of hope and was delivered by themselves as well as many Celestial beings of light, who influenced and became involved in the writing of the book.

Michael and Sarah now spend time being guests on many radio stations in the UK and USA, attend many mind body and spirit events signing their books, write articles for a number of well-respected magazines within their genres as well as give talks on their topics of passion. They also write and send out regular newsletters for their ever growing number of dedicated subscribers and offer advice and support for those who visit them, all through their increasingly popular website.

Now Michael and Sarah wish to present their second book *Beyond The Illusion - A Time Of Awakening*, in order to continue to open people's eyes to the hidden truths and unlimited possibilities of our world. They again spread a message of hope and encouragement and most of all, shine their light to help others along the way on their own paths, something that is greatly needed in these current times of transition here on Earth.

This twin flame Husband and Wife team are passionate about helping others to awaken their true potentials, to reactivate their spiritual enlightenment and ultimately to shine their own light upon our planet Earth, as we all realise our own special parts in team humanity and beyond.

We are all '*spiritual beings*' having a 'human' experience. We just need to remember who we are and why we volunteered to incarnate into this physical embodiment at this uniquely important time.

Michael and Sarah are in the process of setting up a centre for those now awakening in order to teach and interact with people and help them to return to nature and their true selves. The centre will initially begin in the heart of the UK but may eventually expand across the globe. The name of this centre is *Earthshine Sanctuary*.

Join Michael and Sarah and see beyond the veil of illusion.

ABOUT THE BOOK

From Astral travels, meetings with the Angels, Earthbound spirits (ghosts), channelled messages from the many Celestial beings to new teachings of the ancient wonders of Egypt; this book has it all.

Not only do Michael and Sarah share with you their many experiences, in this, their second book of this nature, they also aim to educate the world to realise that as a human race we are being controlled and manipulated and prevented from being the all possibility that is truly us.

Fake wars, deliberate diverted focus, analysing the things that are superficially different about us in order to force us to police ourselves. Circumstances caused to keep us enslaved and controlled and at a low vibrational level, and all to keep *you* from knowing what the system knows about reality and its manipulation.

Michael and Sarah explain that society and those behind the scenes, what many would call the secret governments, actually take massive steps to keep you from knowing about the enlightenment that is you and all of us. Michael and Sarah have detailed how this is done and how you can counteract the effects as you strive to become the real all knowing, all seeing you. Examples of this manipulation include the food that we eat, the water that we drink, the medicines we administer to ourselves and many others. Furthermore there are a few surprises as to the other measures being taken by our so called leaders, these will shock you.

As you become aware of the truth of this situation it empowers you to act against it, knowledge is your power.

This is what those in control do not want you to know. Michael and Sarah have had much resistance from these forces along their journey who have tried at all costs to delay them and stop their messages getting out to you the people. They have failed and the message has finally reached you, the masses.

This book will empower you but more importantly it will give you the tools to see through the illusion that you are kept within and help you to realise the true you.

It has become a passion to both Michael and Sarah to help as many people as possible to see this fact. As Michael and Sarah would say "*We are all a spiritual being having a human experience*". Let's make the most of our gifted experience and become the wonderful beings of light we came here to become. We are *free*; we are all '*one*'

Both Michael and Sarah played an equal part in the writing of this second book, which will become apparent as it is read, but their individual and unique styles compliment each other's and the actual message of the words themselves. Sarah has contributed some of her visionary and channelled artwork throughout this book.

Join Michael and Sarah in their experiences and share in the knowledge that belongs to everyone.

Let's go... Beyond The Illusion - A Time Of Awakening.

CHAPTER 1:

The Planetary Illusion And Beyond

The world isn't what you think it is. The world isn't what you have been led to believe it is. The world is much more beautiful and graceful than we could ever currently realise, but in its current physical state it is accurate to say that there is a lot of work to be done and changes that need to be made; for the better. And the chances are, by virtue of the fact that you are reading this book, you are one of the very beings to do it; much more, you likely volunteered to be on the planet at this time for that very purpose.

Do you ever wonder what life is really about? Who you really are and why you are really here? Do you feel within you that there is so much more 'out there', that there must be, because existence is far too complicated to be a coincidence? Deep within your being you know this to be true. The idea that we are born, to grow up, to go into 'education', to go into further 'education', to get a job, to pay our taxes, to get a mortgage, to spend most of our lives working to pay off that mortgage and other debts, to then die and that be the end of that, is, in our eyes, completely outrageous.

We know from experience that this is quite simply, not the case. You see we have been on a journey. All our lives we have been on a journey and every single moment of every single day has led us to the point that we currently reside in our lives. We realise now that we are spirit having a human experience and not the other way round. We have been conscious of this fact for a few years now and looking back we can see that our lives are now unrecognisable since we made this discovery. We are spirit at this time having a human experience and when you realise this, there is nowhere to hide! You cannot bury your head in the sand hoping that everything will stay the same. How can it when you have discovered this monumental fact? The realisation that there is more to life, more to living, more to you, is a triumph when all the odds are stacked against you and all the big guns aimed in your direction. The best thing to do from that point on is to 'go with the flow' as they say, for if you struggle against it, that is what life becomes; a struggle. Instead it is better to embrace the knowledge of this new found reality and trust that what follows is divinely ordered. Sometimes it can feel as though your life is falling apart, that everything you've worked for is splitting in two, but very often this is the process of transformation. It can be a blessing in disguise and therefore for your highest good. The old, non-serving ways must first dissolve so that the big beautiful butterfly can emerge. And emerge it will.

This happened for us in a relatively short period of time. Mick and I were both frontline police officers, based in the same area of the UK. We joined this job at different times but both for the very same reason; we wanted to help people. We wanted to be the ones to bring justice for those that had been genuinely wronged and to prevent people from being victims. And this at times we managed to do. However, after a combined service to the community of 21 years, our 'careers' came to an abrupt end. Don't worry, we weren't given the proverbial boot! This was completely by choice.

Michael & Sarah in their police days

We had had a major spiritual awakening and with this a much needed reality check. We wrote in our book, *Walk Into The Light – The Journey Of A Lightworker Duo*, about our experiences with the ghost of Sarah Jenson, a Victorian teenager that had been murdered by her Stepfather in 1850. This girl had been a spirit attachment around the two of us and had been trying to get our attention for some time. One morning she did just that. Both of us woke up in the early hours of one February morning and were screaming hysterically. This took place seemingly on another dimension as what I clearly remember happening to Mick, is what Mick clearly remembers happening to me. I saw Mick screaming as if being attacked and whilst trying to calm him down found that he was unresponsive to me and instead looked through me as if I weren't there. Mick's experience on the other hand was the opposite way round, him trying to calm me for example. Very confusing I know but we know now that this took place on another level and later on found out that we were reliving the murder of our spirit friend.

This was a traumatising experience for both of us and one which took us both a little while to recover from, so much so that we had to take time out to let the emotional trauma of what we had been through, heal. This event was a major eye opener for both of us and one which made us question once and for all what it was we wanted from our lives. The answer to that was love, truth, happiness and freedom. Freedom to live, freedom to express, freedom to just be whatever we desired to be. We had already started to become aware that things just weren't right in the world.

We had started to feel like a slave to our job, slave to our debts and mortgage, unhappy with it all but unable to see a way out. Even closer to home, we realised that the job we had dedicated ourselves to, wasn't as honourable as we may have first thought. How could it be when first hand we saw with our own eyes crime figures being manipulated on a computer screen in order to suit the organisation and then to see these falsities presented to the public and the manipulator being rewarded with a cash bonus for doing so, or as they prefer to define it 'crime management'. How could we provide a service to people when they were calling for help one day, and then that help not being dispatched until three days later due to having 'no-one to send'? Not enough regard for safety, wheels dropping off police cars due to lack of care and proper maintenance, being told not to target those known to be carrying drugs but instead those going about their days causing no nuisance to anyone else, officers being prevented from doing a good job because of 'red tape' and bureaucracy. These are just a few of the things that go on within these kinds of organisations. There is much more we could tell you but needless to say that we felt that the whole thing was lacking integrity when the force itself would often make an example of individuals for issues of integrity! This to us just all seemed backwards and still does, as with most systems in today's society. That was it; we could not endorse the 'service' anymore. We had to leave.

With this and everything else that had taken place we made the decision to leave our careers as police officers. By now we were also waking up to what was really going on in the world and realised how nearly everything was geared towards stopping people from finding out who they really are and what they are capable of, the fact that we are spiritual beings having a human experience and have abilities beyond our wildest dreams, capable of changing the world for the better, literally overnight. Capable of telepathic communication, of instant manifestation, able to de-materialise from one place and re-materialise somewhere else, miraculous healing, levitation, you name it, we can all do it. Maybe not right now at this very moment, but the potential is there, lying dormant until such a time we are able to access it again, when we are responsible and use these things for the highest good of all and not for the gain of self. Although there are those still living today that have dedicated themselves to the path of self-discovery and are able to perform these feats.

Humanity on the whole, has allowed itself to be convinced that it is nothing special, that our lives should only consist of the 'normal', mundane routines that society at the time dictates. We have become reliant on the state, exactly as planned to lure people into a false sense of security and to make them helpless otherwise, whilst those at the 'top' reap the monetary and other rewards for our efforts. The majority of people will get an education then move onto a job and work for the rest of their lives to pay off their debts and support their families. What kind of a 'life' is that? Is that what we came here for... to be a slave to the system? Is this the kind of life you imagined for you and your children? We have become accepting of our bar-less prisons and are happy to function within it so long as it gets us by.

We, as well as many other respected individuals, are trying to let people know that this is not the way it was intended to be. When we look back into history there is talk of various 'Golden ages' where everyone lived in full awareness of who they were and functioned 'as one', where everyone acted with love and integrity towards one another, where all existed together and worked as a community for the highest good of all. There was no money, no system that allowed the few to be more wealthy than most could ever dream of and left others lacking as a result. The people worked for each other and were not bribed to do so for monetary rewards. They did it because they cared and as a result everyone was considered equal. Do you think that if all of a sudden money ceased to exist, that the Earth would stop turning? Of course it wouldn't! There were no food and water shortages, no-one would go hungry and no-one would ever want for anything. The Earth was not raped of her resources and lived in harmony with the people and the people in harmony with the Earth. They did not need to rely on technology as everything they could ever need was within them, they used their infinite abilities when necessary and sometimes for the fun of it but always for the highest good of all. We can, and will, ascend to this level of awareness again. But certain barriers and obstructions must first be dissolved and transmuted.

Our real and purest state of being is that of infinite awareness, eternal consciousness and high vibratory beings. The more you expand your consciousness and your awareness, the higher your very being vibrates. Everything has a different level of vibration or frequency. The higher your frequency, the more consciously aware you are and the more light that shines from and through you. The lower the frequency, the less consciously aware and the less light that shines forth. High frequency emotions include those of love, joy, laughter, happiness, respect and integrity. Low frequency emotions include hate, anger, selfishness, jealousy and the one that is used against us the most; fear. When your energy is highly vibrant, life flows much easier and you are able to create and live much more in alignment with your own soul. Everything is clearer and you feel physically well within yourself. This kind of high energy can also literally inspire your physical and emotional bodies to heal themselves of any dis-ease in turn creating more positive energy. The opposite can be said when you feel constantly negative and emotionally drained.

Why is it then, that most of the events that take place in the world today all seem to be of a negative, fearful nature? Is it by complete coincidence that all around the world we seem to be undergoing the same problems, finding corrupt politicians, corrupt bankers, economic disasters, natural disasters, terrorism and so on and so forth? We can tell you this; it is no coincidence. It is by design. There are those in this world (but not necessarily of it), that do not have our best interests at heart. They work through their inter-connected governmental puppets, organisations and corporations to gain complete control over humanity's every affair. They work tirelessly to continually create negative situations to bring about bad low vibrational energies which they for one, feed off and to secondly prevent humanity from accessing higher levels of energy and therefore awareness of who we really are.

We are kept distracted by the not so independent media corporations and are drip fed what to believe from a very early age. We are given false versions of history and are fed drama after drama with one thing and another, be it the ever popular celebrity culture, television soap operas, game shows and more. It is okay to enjoy these things so long as we don't make them the centre focus of our attention. Toxic chemicals in our food, poisons such as fluoride in our water, genetically modified organisms that we're not told about, vaccines to damage our immune systems, mercury that is poisonous to all living things contained in the new fluorescent 'energy saving' light bulbs as well as in tooth fillings, false flag terrorism events; all things that are used to keep humanity locked into a low vibrational state to maintain the low dense energies that they feed off, but all things that we can easily overcome with awareness.

All this to keep us from ever looking up! And why? Because if we ever realise as a whole who we are and what we are doing here, then those in their illusory positions of power over humanity, will lose it. They will be, and are being, exposed for what they really are and will thereby be liable for some kind of compensation (not the monetary type) but more likely that of Karma to balance out the wrongs that they have committed.

We are kept in a constant state of worry over making sure we pay the bills on time, making sure we pay the mortgage on time, (which by the way literally means 'death grip'), then there is taxation, the mighty web. Taxation is a legal requirement in society dating back to our earliest days, legal because the recipients of this tax say so. In the UK it is hard to see what our taxes have contributed to. We pay road tax, but the roads are so full of pot holes it sometimes feels that we need a lunar carrier! Then we pay to park on a road because there is a little white box that tells you to, or else! Public transport that is often late, regularly breaks down and is continually more expensive than going by car, and yet is sold to us as a viable alternative to save on carbon emissions and as a consequence, 'global warming', all in aid of a new form of carbon tax!

We pay national insurance in the UK but often wait hours to see a doctor. Care can be sub-zero due to lack of doctors, nurses and time. Dentist appointments can take weeks and we still pay despite paying national insurance. Fuel prices continue to rise and we are told that oil is now a rare commodity, when we know that if people believe something is running out then they will pay more for it as a result. It is the 'peak oil myth'. Energy bills are increasing to such an extent that our senior citizens are dying in the cold because they cannot afford to switch on their heating when energy companies are enjoying record multi-billion pound annual profits from this naturally recurring commodity?

It seems that everyone, especially so called 'authority', has constantly got its hand in your wallet. In January of 2011 in the UK, Valued Added Tax (V.A.T) went up to 20%, the highest in UK history, to allegedly help pay for the financial deficit our country finds itself in due to the global financial ruin engineered by the banks. We could be forgiven for saying that we've already paid for that once with a multi-billion pound tax payer bailout, so why are we paying for it a second time with further tax increases and cuts in public services? Incidentally the cuts and scarcity we face are to save seven billion pounds and yet banker's bonuses for the period 2010/2011 have been announced to be that very amount! We see a simple solution here. Did you know that those in charge of insurance companies actually have masonic style meetings to discuss how they can avoid paying insurance claims? Did you realise that when you register something it becomes state owned, Regis = King and this dates back to our ancient times too and it still remains today. And more to the point the system legislates against you so that you have no choice but to register it or face prosecution, they have all angles covered. Hook line and sinker comes to mind. Did you know that you have to have permission to protest against the British government anywhere near the British parliament? Free speech at its best!

All the while our millionaire leaders, who remain unaffected by the hardships they and their masters decree we must face, go unaffected. We are currently entrapped in this situation as it is woven around us in order to keep us worrying from one pay cheque to the next. Scarcity equals dependency and dependency equals control. This is where we have fallen victim, given our power away when we held the key all of the time (and still do).

Does all this sound like something infinite consciousness would choose?

The illusion is ever so apparent when it comes to politics and the faces that represent each individual party. It doesn't matter what this party or that party says they are going to do if elected to government, because they all end up doing the same. We have had some spectacular U-turns in the most recent election in the UK where parties beforehand claimed they would do A, B and C. What happened? They did the same as the last government did! All parties claiming to be in opposition with each other and one saying they will do this and the other saying they will do that. Whatever happens, they always pick up where the previous government left off, despite their outlandish promises to win your vote. They carry on with the agenda that was inherent before they stepped up to the podium. We are led to believe that we have a choice of who to vote for, but in reality you are given the choice that those maintaining the agenda want you to have. This is not freedom! *This is an illusion.* You are being led to believe that you have a choice. You can only exercise your freewill if you have a choice. Many fall into a cycle of saying that the last government didn't work because of the previous leader, and the one before that didn't work because of the leader and the government before that which was a different party didn't work because of the leader. Surely people can see that the leaders are merely the puppets for an agenda that continues on the same, no matter who is at the helm? As the saying goes, *"It doesn't matter who you vote for, the government always gets in"*! So true.

Many tactics are used to keep us from becoming a united force, 'divide and rule' being a main player. If we are busy at competition with each other, this again becomes a distraction, something to keep us busy and occupied so that our minds don't start to wander. For example, at work as police officers there was once an amazing team spirit. Everyone worked as a team, no one was ever left behind and everyone went home happy at the end of the day. Then came the introduction of competition. First it was competition between different stations of the same command centre. Then came competition between individual teams of that command centre. And then this was followed by competition of individuals leading people to strive for the most arrests, most crime detections and therefore the best figures. This bred a generation of robot officers and in turn dislodged team spirit to instead replace it with a selfish 'as long as I'm okay' attitude. The place went downhill from there.

Racism is another powerful example of divide and rule. We tend to focus on our differences instead of what unites us, what it is that makes us human. Disliking someone because of the colour of their skin is as crazy as disliking someone for having a different coloured car to you! After all, our fleshy bodies are our vehicles for experiencing 'life' in this reality. Sure there may be certain things about a certain culture that you don't like or agree with but that is no reason to dislike a whole race of people. The wonderful thing about freewill is that we are free to choose how we express ourselves. We all do this in different ways. As long as we don't enforce this upon others it isn't a problem. We go by the motto 'Live and let live'.

As we bring the first chapter to a close it is important to realise that we are all the same, yet at the same time we are all different. This may sound like a paradox but our divine essence is the same. Each of us are divine sparks of consciousness separated from the cosmic central consciousness that is at the centre of everything, the very essence from which we were all created. Some choose to call this 'God'. Yet when we incarnate to a certain place or planet, in this case Earth, we choose to express ourselves in different ways. This is good, we are all connected but having our own experience. It would be pretty boring if we all came and did exactly the same thing and had exactly the same experiences! We need variety. We have a lot we can teach each other and a lot we can learn from each other. Just take what resonates within you and leave behind what doesn't. Hence, we are the same but different.

What we have outlined here is the illusion. The illusion that we were born to work and struggle through life, the illusion that we are free and have a genuine choice when it comes to choosing our 'leaders', the illusion that we don't have any power and that we are nothing more than sheeple. The illusion that we are helpless and that there is nothing we can do to change things. Oh how we can change it, by coming together and working as ONE. This illusion is starting to crumble before our very eyes as people begin to awaken from their slumber. No longer will there be any holding us back. We have so much Love and support in our mission from other places, but the illusion that has been built up over many thousands of years is throwing everything at us in a desperate attempt to remain in control; it is doomed. And now it is being dismantled piece by piece.

In the coming years it is going to become more and more apparent that we are all on the same team; team cosmos! And we will need to play our part with so much love and integrity as a united force. Love, or Level Of Vibrational Energy, is the answer to everything. If we hold true love for all our fellow man and every living thing in the energy centre of our hearts, then we will turn this planet around in no time. No violence necessary. Think about it; if we all loved each other like one of our own, then how could the thought of hurting one another possibly enter our heads? It just wouldn't. We would want the best for each other and what's more, we wouldn't accept anything less.

That time is coming. Will you be ready?

CHAPTER 2:

Death Is Just The Start

Born to live, we live to die. Well at least that's what we are led to believe, filled with fear that death is the end of us forever. What we can say without any personal doubt is that death is just the start, the start of the next part of your soul journey. There are so many true accounts and stories from all walks of life who recite experiences with ghosts and alike. So with so many things now being reported how can these events not be true? When you or anyone sees a ghost what are you looking at? Putting it simply you are looking at a former physical incarnation that has parted company with its physical body at the point of physical death. The being is now a non-physical form bearing the same features, the same characteristics and even the same personality as they once did, that's why when family or friends come back to visit us we can instantly recognise them. They are still alive, just not physically alive. They are still a living consciousness that exists in dimensions different to our own, but they have the ability and the know how to cross and pass through these dimensional vortex's, seemingly when they choose to.

So this being the case, how can we subscribe to the spoken fear and belief system that teaches us that at death you are no more when such overwhelming evidence to the contrary exists and that this evidence is becoming almost just the norm these days? More and more television programs about the so called supernatural and paranormal seem to be on our screens and so many people are actually seeing it for themselves as well as often catching some of this bizarre activity on camera. To us, this is fantastic evidence that there is something more out there, something beyond what we currently know or are being told.

Sarah and I recently went to Jersey in the British Channel Islands for a short break. Jersey was in the second world war occupied by German forces and on the first evening in our hotel room, which was an area once concentrated by German troops, Sarah and I could sense a non-physical female presence in the room. This presence we felt, was staring at us with a strong sense of curiosity but not out to cause us any harm. I could see her in my third eye (psychic eye) and invited her over from the far side of the room to where Sarah and I were sitting. She came over and sat on a nearby stool. I had a telepathic conversation with her whereby she told me that she was 25 years of age when she died in 1943. She told me that her name was Hayley which she spelt out for me; H-a-y-l-e-y. Hayley said that she was part of the Jersey resistance during the German occupation. I had researched the Jersey resistance during a previous trip to the islands a couple of years earlier, so I knew that it did exist and that the information being received was accurate.

Hayley told me that the Germans had somehow found out that she was part of the resistance and that she had been shot as a result of this. The area where our room was situated was where she used to hide from the occupying forces. She began to show to me mental images of the German forces on the island and I could feel her agitation. I told her that the war had been won in 1945 by the British forces and that the island of Jersey had been liberated, a fact that she was not aware of. I told her that she should be very proud of herself because it was people like her that had helped with the victory and actual liberation; she had played a big role just like many other members of the resistance had by standing up against the oppression of an invading force.

I could feel her relief as she was informed of this fact. I asked her if she wanted to be taken into the light after both Sarah and I had explained to her exactly what the light was. After a short time we could sense that Hayley had been taken through the light by my spirit guides who were also around us. Just before Hayley left I could sense her alongside me, as if giving me a peck on the right cheek, saying *"thank you"*. Following this, the room felt initially empty and lacking as this spirit was no longer occupying the same physical space as ourselves, which was blatantly obvious to both Sarah and I. It is a real honour to be able to do this kind of thing and we will forever treasure the memory of meeting someone who had passed during the war, who we didn't even know had existed until now. Hayley will now be in the place her vibration and soul belong. Bless her memory.

This was a moving story and one that gives us a clue as to what may be going on around us. This was an innocent holiday for us and yet we found ourselves accompanied by the spirit of a young woman from days that had long vanished, in Earth terms anyway.

I have had a number of family and friends who have left this physical realm come and speak to me, telling me that they are okay and that they passed to the 'other side' without any problems. To Sarah and I, we no longer think of death as the end, to us it is just another reality and the next step in our continual evolutionary expansion of consciousness. This gives us so much comfort to know.

Even famous historical figures return. I can remember such an occasion near to our home in a 15th century building, seeing King Charles I (Bonnie Prince Charlie) appear and walk from one side of the room to the other before disappearing. He was dressed in a burgundy cavalier outfit, with a cavalier hat and still had the features I had seen in many pictures of him, including a lot of facial hair. It turned out that this area was where he occasionally used to stay when he was king all those centuries ago. I also learned that he liked to return now and again even in these modern times. What was strange is that he was beheaded for treason in 1498, but when I saw him he definitely still had his head attached to the rest of him! The sighting lasted about ten seconds from beginning to end.

In the latter part of 2010 a good friend of mine took his own life, it seems that he couldn't come to terms with the bad memories of some of the horrid things he had experienced and seen during his working life. I had known him since the early 1990's when we worked together in the police force. He has since visited me twice and although he appears younger than when I last saw him in the physical, he looks the same as when I knew him as a physical person. He told me during the two separate occasions that I telepathically spoke to him, that he was now in a good place and we then continued with a general chat, although fairly short it was good to catch up with him. We talked about the police force and why I had left, a fact that I never actually got to tell him about before he died, and of course a few other things regarding the ending of his physical life. Now I had the chance to say some of the things I never got to say before, and I made the most of this brief moment. My friend then walked up to me and patted the top of my head and disappeared just as quickly as he had appeared. A moment I will always remember and treasure. We have all lost someone close to us, but be assured that they are never far away from you, wherever you are. Whatever you do, they watch over you, just as they did when they walked this realm with us.

This is also relevant to our pets and all other animals and mammals, in fact every living thing. They too have an evolutionary path and incarnate into the bodies of animals in order to learn and grow just like the souls of the evolutionary path of the human does. And once they leave their own physical animal bodies their soul goes to a dimension and realm that caters for them and their needs, again just as human souls do.

I have had, and have heard of a number of experiences where pets of ours, who have long since left this realm, have come back to visit us. I have in many meditations had two of my pet dogs, a Border Collie and a West Highland Terrier, appear to me and once one of them was seen by physical eyes running across the conservatory floor towards me. My Mother has seen, with her physical eyes, both of these dogs walking down the hallway of her flat. My Stepfather has been awoken on a few occasions to the barking of the same West Highland Terrier and when calling him, in the same vain as when he was a physical pet, a picture fell off the wall, as the energy of excitement spiralled throughout his bedroom, like a whirlwind just below the ceiling. They are both continually hearing his collar as he walks around the flat, making that metallic jingling noise, just as it did when he was physically there with them. This may seem strange on the face of it, but I have also channelled messages from the West Highland Terrier, meant for my parents, which were duly passed on. Because once we leave the physical, language is not a barrier to us and telepathic communication can occur, just as when we talk amongst ourselves in everyday life.

We have so much help and support around us in the form of Spirit guides and others which we come to later. If everyone only knew this fact they would be much happier and feel so much more comforted. We are not alone and *you* are not alone, together we have a brilliant team behind us. We are all part of the universal 'Oneness' that is everything and we are all connected together in ways that would absolutely stun you. We are all existence in many different forms. WE ARE!

We hope that this chapter has comforted you and helped you to realise that death is not the end; it is just the start. Life is about learning, loving and overcoming and facing fears of all kinds. Death is by far one of the biggest fear obstacles placed in our way, not only by others but by ourselves. The fear of death in its many forms can hold you back in a number of ways and can prevent you from living your life to its fullest potential. For some, it can be almost paralysing, having people afraid to live life because of death! We need to release our fears about death and all the worries that it brings, to the universe. We're not saying have little or no regard for life or safety but simply not to allow ourselves to be imprisoned by the idea of death. We are spirit in a human body and we can NEVER die. Life is a gift, an opportunity to become increasingly and more consciously aware of who we are and then to use this to reach the highest heights of 'life' with love in our hearts. We can achieve literally anything if we were in touch with and aware of who and what we really are. On some planets in our magnificent and endless universe and indeed universes, both physical and non-physical, the departure of a soul through death is celebrated! It is seen that the soul who has departed was ready for the next level, the next stage in their development and so their 'life' would be celebrated and all that they had achieved. We're not saying that whenever someone here passes we should be happy about it and jump for joy! Definitely not. It is still and possibly always will be an upsetting occasion for most as it is for us. But instead of dwelling so much on the death of the individual, it can be beneficial and comforting to remember their 'life' and to know that they're not really gone. Nothing is ever lost in the eyes of the universe and as Archangel Michael once said to me *"enjoy your time there on Earth, you have an eternity to be elsewhere"*.

We have on many occasions been to a local forest and have cleared many lost souls that were stuck in limbo upon the Earth plane, returning them, with the help of the Angelic realm, through into the light (See pictures overleaf). This is an absolute honour to participate in. There is so much activity around us, most of it invisible to our physical eyes but nevertheless it is there; beauty and life as we *don't know it*, trying to connect and be with us.

We see on nearly every occasion tree spirits, orbs and ghostly figures moving in between the forest as well as ectoplasm, ghostly mists and as you will see in the pictures overleaf the Angelic realm both protecting and helping us to gather and clear lost souls to get them on their way to the next appropriate level.

Orbs can be many things, but basically are a vehicle for the spirit realm. They can be lost souls, Angels, Ascended Masters, Elementals, Intergalactic beings, animals and even souls that are yet to incarnate just waiting for their communion with a physical body. When we clear these souls we also help planet Earth, by virtue of the fact that the lingering energy can cause an energetic drain upon Earth itself. This can be likened to a thorough cleansing.

This to Sarah and I proves the existence of life after physical death. We have seen it, it is real and it is life in another fashion. We have photographic evidence to prove it. To Sarah and I death is not the end, it is just the start.

Protection from Archangel Michael – Bright orb top right

Bright Angel orbs, assisting many lost souls into the light

In the next chapter we will look in more detail about what happens with the light and a soul's a passing, but to bring this chapter to a close we would like to leave you with this quote:

"To fear death, my friends, is only to think ourselves wise, without being wise: for it is to think that we know what we do not know. For anything that men can tell, death may be the greatest good that can happen to them: but they fear it as if they knew quite well that it was the greatest of evils. And what is this but that shameful ignorance of thinking that we know what we do not know"?

- Socrates (BC 469-BC 399) Greek philosopher of Athens

CHAPTER 3:

The Light - A Passage To Infinity

Many people often speak of a beautiful light that is present at the point of leaving the body following physical death. Many people have had near death experiences and found themselves walking through this tunnel of light, often greeted by those they had known and lost in their physical lives, only then to be told that it isn't their time and that they must turn back. To witness this kind of event at a hospital for example is deemed simply amazing; even a miracle as the person had been pronounced dead only to spring back to life after several minutes.

So what is *the light* and when you die do you have to go into it? Well first of all, the light itself is like a portal, a gateway to the next phase of a soul's journey. It literally transports from the current reality of the three dimensional Earth plane to another dimension, the next stage in the journey; that being appropriate to whatever level of development the individual has progressed to. As for whether you have to go through it, well the answer is quite simply "no". Just as when you are 'alive' and kicking on the Earth plane you are born with freewill. So it is when you die. You can choose not to go into the light and instead elect to stay on the three dimensional Earth plane. However, this is not advisable as to do so you need a constant supply of energy and as you now don't possess a physical body or vessel to get around in, you have to literally steal that energy from somewhere (or someone) else. You would also just be putting off the next natural step of your soul journey. Individuals that elect to stay on the Earth in this way are referred to as 'ghosts' or 'Earthbound spirits'. They are also said to be walking the Earth in limbo.

There are numerous reasons for these spirits making such a decision, such as they were too scared to go through the light and didn't know what would happen. They were angry to have died and refused to move on, they didn't want to leave behind their families, didn't want to let go of their material possessions and decided that if they couldn't take it with them then they weren't going either! This is why some objects are said to be haunted such as cars and antique furniture. Some feel they have not had justice for the way they died and stay to seek revenge or bring out the truth. The list goes on but needless to say that you are definitely in control of your decision when you pass on. This we know from much research as well as our own experiences.

Earthbound spirits have to utilise energy from their surroundings to be able to exist and function in the physical world. This energy very often comes from human emotions particularly that of the negative kind, such as fear, anger, stress, sadness and depression etc. This is because these emotions are more resonant to the Earthbound spirit. They can, and very often do, create situations to cause a certain reaction from people which the spirit then proceeds to feed off to keep going. For example, they can cause a computer to crash just by standing by it; they can on occasion move things or cause people to snap for no reason and they can generally create a negative atmosphere around the home and other places. We believe that this is quite often the cause of relationship breakdowns and unnecessary arguments as the unsuspecting couples and families fall victim to the ghost's energy trap. It may be wise to consider this if you feel you may have a spirit in the house or at work for example, that way you can stay one step ahead and not react in a certain way to a given situation of the negative kind.

What happens when the spirit doesn't get the energy they need is they wind down to such a degree that they could be likened to a flat battery. Mediums have actually seen such cases where the spirit has occupied an empty house for many years with no energy to feed from and they have been reduced to a heap in a corner, unable to do anything. Although, these spirits can be annoying and at times very frightening in what they do and cause to happen, we can help them and thereby help ourselves. We have had first-hand experience of this and had we not of had such a strong bond, would likely have fallen victim to the spirits concerned; see *Walk Into The Light – The Journey Of A Lightworker Duo*. If you have a ghost problem and you would like it to be resolved then we suggest the best thing to do would be to contact an experienced medium, who is used to working with spirits and also energy so that they can help the ghost to go into the light and then place further love, healing and protective energy around you and your home or problem area. You need someone who is able to converse directly with the spirit and not just flick holy water at them!

So we've covered what happens when someone chooses not to go into the light now let's look at what happens when you do go through into the light.

The light is a doorway to the next stage of natural soul progression. Remember that you have come to the Earth and incarnated into a physical body for the experience. Your soul is constantly learning, growing, expanding in consciousness and awareness of itself. It has been reported that when you go through the light, you end up in a place that is vibrationally compatible to you. What we mean by this is that if you in your experience as a soul so far and following your Earthly life have developed to such a degree that you are a good person, well-meaning and intentioned and most importantly have love in your heart, even if you made some mistakes along the way, then it is safe to say that your vibratory rate is going to be pretty good. Therefore your soul will gravitate to a place of similar frequency and your experience is likely to be a good one. In complete contrast however, there are souls out there who, putting it quite mildly, have been nothing but plain evil. They may not have allowed real love into their existences and have done some appalling things during their time. You may have heard the phrase 'we create our own reality'? Well we do quite literally and for these darker souls their vibrations are of a very low density and what we would say of a negative frequency. Therefore they would naturally gravitate to the lower levels and murky depths of the astral planes where their vibrations would be comfortable and able to withstand the lower density. All souls though, whatever 'level' they occupy are able to learn, grow and progress to the next stage once they have learned and gleaned what they need from their current experience.

There are many levels of the astral planes which surround us, all existing at the same time and occupying the same 'space'. Think of the astral as the many different layers of dimensions that exist around us. There are the higher levels which are said to be so beautiful that they can be likened to Heaven and have 'Heavenly beings' including the Angels and then there are the lower levels which are the opposite and are therefore likened to Hell with its low vibrational entities and its Hellish creations. There is beyond the astral for the advanced soul but most are working their way through the astral levels at this time. So when we talk about creating our own realities you could say that every breath we take and every move we make right now is preparing our place here on the Earth and thereafter. We are moulding 'the Now', the present moment, and although this can be a long and arduous task at the current density here on the physical Earth, the vibrations are lifting and are starting to change the world.

From others experiences, it is said that there are stopping off stations once you pass through the light and wake up on the 'other side'. These stations are like hospitals (but not our Earthly ones) where there are loving souls dedicated to nursing the 'new arrivals' back to comfort. These souls can be people you have known in 'life' and they will help the new arrival come to terms with the fact that they have withdrawn from the physical and died a physical death. They will assist the soul in coming to terms with any mistakes made during the preceding 'life' and in some cases help them to make contact with family members still 'living'. The carers will also make sure that you are reunited with others that passed before you. These stations are said to be so peaceful and tranquil that some are even happy to remain there and believe them to be Heaven. One thing a soul must do at this point is to go through their divine blueprint or 'life plan'. This is the plan you set out before incarnating into your human body (or even the non-human body for that matter) and is kind of like a checklist of things that you set out to achieve and experience during your 'life'. Some find during the review that they did quite well and others find they veered completely off path but nonetheless still learned a lot from doing so. Higher beings can also be present with you during this event to help you through.

Once the soul is ready and able, they then begin to gravitate towards their next stage which normally leads them back to their soul groups who often reside on higher planes. The soul group is a family of beings who work together to progress through the process of soul evolution together. Sometimes some of the group incarnate at the same time into physical lives and when these souls come together during that life they are said to be 'soul mates'. The soul mate relationship doesn't necessarily have to be an intimate relationship either. The rest of the group will continue with their path in the ethereal realms and await your return. Together you share your various experiences and this is how the group progresses. Within a soul group you also get much more closely, energetically connected members and they are referred to as 'twin flames'. It is rare for twin flames to incarnate together in the physical but it does happen and currently seems to be rising in number, again we can attest to this.

So as you can see, existence is a continual path of growth and experience from one realm to the next. It's up to you; you can either choose to refuse the inevitable and remain in your own self-made prison (here or on the 'other side') or you can choose to go where the energy flow takes you, onto the next phase of your evolutionary path and towards a lighter existence.

Not to confuse things here, but this is all just one aspect of the 'real' us, the infinite consciousness, and that means that we can exist and experience in several places at once and that includes on other planets and dimensions. Remember that we are limitless beings capable of anything and although this may seem impossible to the rational, logical mind, we are far greater than we are led to believe.

For those who have read *Walk into the Light - The Journey Of A Lightworker Duo,* you will be familiar with the Sarah Jenson story already mentioned in chapter 1. She was a Victorian girl from 1850 who had been murdered by her stepfather. She had been a spirit attachment to both of us for several years until we relived her death and eventually sent her into the light having revealed her story to the world. Sarah Jenson has 'popped' back to reconvene with us since her eventual passing into the light. This would be like popping to see a friend or relative at their home to see how they were doing. One such visit took place at about 10pm in September of 2010. Sarah Jenson appeared to Mick and I in our third eye (psychic eye energy centre located between the eyebrows). Mick could see her standing in the lounge dressed in a pink and lilac dress, appearing very happy and at peace which was a beautiful thing, given the 'life' she had undertaken here on Earth. Mick recalls the following conversation with her:

(Sarah J) – *"I'm sorry for what I put you through, but I'm happy now"*.

(Mick) "Don't be sorry, if it wasn't for you we wouldn't be where we are now, we are where we are because of you. How's John"? (John was the stepfather who we referred to, who was also attached to us)

(Sarah J) *"I don't really know"*.

(Mick) "Are you a Spirit guide for anyone at the moment"?

(Sarah J) *"No not at the moment, I am free to come and go as I please"*.

(Mick) "Do you mind us letting your story out in the book"?

(Sarah J) *"No I don't mind my story getting out, it's going to be big"*.

(Mick) "Is there anything you would like me to say to Sarah"?

(Sarah J) *"Just thank you and I will keep popping back"*.

Sarah Jenson then walked to the sofa and sat down. Mick could feel her gently touching the top of his head and we could smell the waft of a beautiful scent pass us by. We could feel a vibrational disturbance within our vicinity and experienced a coolness and tingling sensation. This can happen when spirit are around. Sarah Jenson has left us many signs since her transition to the light to let us know that wherever she now resides, she is well. A happy ending we are pleased to say.

The two of us have been extremely fortunate to have actually seen the light for real with our physical eyes (from this side of the veil)! Not only that, but someone, somewhere also made sure that we got the event on camera.

We, along with our friend Geoff, often take night walks through a nearby forest and place of local beauty. We are all sensitive to the fact that there is much more going on around us than we can see with our own eyes although on occasion we are able to 'tune in' to such a degree as to catch a glimpse of this mysterious world and its inhabitants.

In October 2010 we took one of our usual routes through the forest. It was pitch black and the atmosphere was one of nervous excitement. We had experienced a number of activities of the supernatural kind on many occasions on this walk and often caught the likes of orbs and other phenomena on camera, but never anything like what we were about to experience. I took photos on my camera phone and had indeed acquired this particular camera phone as we felt we may need it for something important. We always asked for protection from the highest light on our expeditions as certain pockets of the forest consisted of unwelcoming and sometimes unfriendly energies.

The three of us had been walking for around 40 minutes and were making our way back when all of a sudden, we saw it. We came to a halt as a massive beam of pure white light, appeared through the trees near where we were stood. It was as though someone had turned on the lights in the forest. The light continued to open up across the road in front of us and none of us could believe what we were seeing. The light remained present for around five or six seconds when suddenly the camera on our phone went off by itself. We were all completely taken aback by what was unfolding before our very eyes and the light was so bright that it was almost difficult to look at. We caught a quick glimpse of the picture that had been taken and could see a beautiful array of white, pinks and purples as well as many orbs that were present. Seconds before, Mick and our companion Geoff had called silently for the help of Archangel Michael, in taking any lost souls in the forest that may have attached themselves to us, into the light. We watched the remainder of the apparition and then ran excitedly back to the entrance of the park. We were breathless and overcome with excitement and complete astonishment. We examined the picture that had been taken and several others we had taken throughout the walk. They were quite simply, stunning. There were a couple of pictures taken before the main event that show what appears to be a doorway of light opening up. However, this doorway was not visible to the naked eye.

A doorway of light opening up behind Mick and unseen to the eye

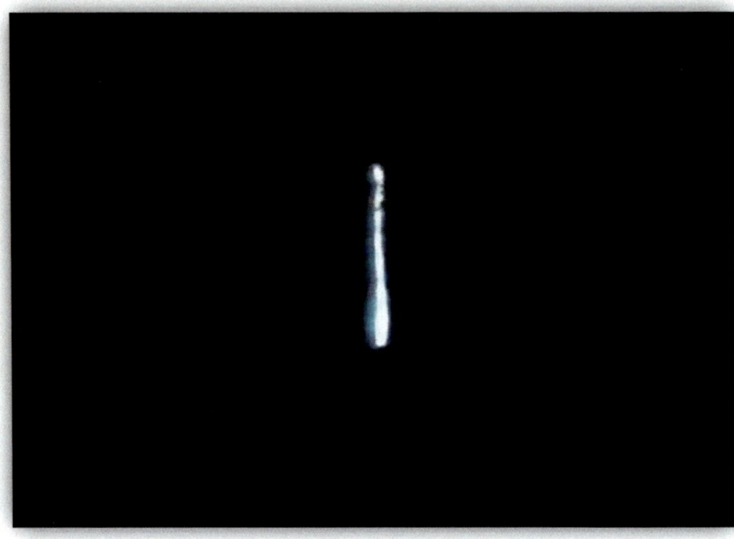

A close up of the opening doorway

The picture that took itself: A bright light with many orbs going into it

We discussed what we had seen and having ruled out any other 'conventional' explanations, came to the conclusion that we had just witnessed *the light* doing it what it does best; providing a gateway to the next phase to those souls ready to take on that journey. And what's more, the picture that took itself, shows exactly that. Furthermore, Mick channelled a short message from Archangel Michael himself that said this: *"I have cleared you of many souls, as you requested, well done and thank you"*.

By now we hope that you feel more confident and reassured that 'death' is not the end and that those that see and talk about the light in the majority of cases, especially those of near death experiences, are speaking the truth. A lot of information has been provided by respected mediums and those that can communicate with the 'dead', that documents their conversations with souls that have passed on. These souls confirm that they are 'alive' and well where they are and that there is more to our existence than many on the Earth plane care to believe. We can confirm from our own experiences, that there is definitely more to life and more to death. There are those who would rather that we remained in fear of death and remain in the belief that there is no point to life. It makes us easier to control.

We are here to say that there is so much more to our very existence full stop, and that there is nothing to fear but fear itself. The light exists and as the years go by, more and more light will shine on the hidden truths of our world.

There is so much to be discovered. Why not open your mind and allow yourself to enjoy the ride. There are some very interesting times ahead.

CHAPTER 4:

Astral Travels

Most human beings have a perception of self that is very limited, one that operates within four walls and doesn't very often like to be challenged. This is changing as more and more people continue to have experiences of a 'supernatural' kind that they cannot explain. But we are capable of things far beyond this reality, things that many would only dream of being real.

Imagine if you could leave your physical body without dying, without having to go through the physical 'death' process and all that it entails, able to be free of all current physical limitations and boundaries set by us or for us. Imagine if you could traverse the universe, learn and experience whilst your physical body remained in the comfort of your own home. Do you believe that such feats are possible? For Mick and I, this is reality. We have both had experiences of the 'out of body' kind where I have on occasions left my physical body (temporarily of course), and Mick has witnessed this phenomenon.

We talked earlier of the astral planes of existence, other dimensions where those that have passed away gravitate to. They will of course gravitate to the particular dimensional plane that their soul is attuned to at that time and where they will be capable of withstanding the vibrations of that particular realm until ready to progress. But you do not need to have departed from the physical to be able to go to, or progress through the levels in this way. We all have the ability to be able to travel in this way using our astral bodies, the non-physical body that allows your consciousness to experience realities beyond this one. When we travel in this way we are said to have performed 'astral projection' or 'astral travel' whereby you are consciously aware of things you encounter while out of your physical body. It is an 'out of body experience' which can be achieved either when you are awake, lucid dreaming or in deep meditation. Astral travelling has been practised for thousands of years and for those that have mastered this process, they are able to travel the stars and beyond, using this to their advantage for soul development. Again you will only be able to move through the many different levels once you have progressed enough to do so. So once again, if you are a negative, nasty, narrow minded individual then you will not be able to access the higher planes. That is because vibrationally, you will not be compatible with the higher energies and frequencies of that level. You have to work on yourself to reach such standards. So astral travel can be used as a tool to your soul development if practised correctly.

I first consciously left my body in 2009 after many years of experiencing sleep paralysis. Sleep paralysis occurs when the physical body is asleep but the conscious mind is wide awake. This can be a terrifying experience when you don't know what is occurring and can lead you to struggle in an attempt to 'wake' yourself up. It seems the more you struggle, the worse it gets so on this particular occasion I decided that I wasn't going to struggle anymore. I was tired of struggling and tired of feeling the immense fear that this would normally bring about. Although initially apprehensive, I managed to stay relatively calm. The next thing I knew, I was sitting up, out of my body and looking down at myself. I couldn't believe it. Mick was lying next to me and I tried to communicate with him but realised that at that moment in time, I would have been like a ghost to him and therefore not heard at that stage. I was shortly pulled back into my physical body by some kind of suctioning motion, before waking physically and sitting up in complete amazement of what had just happened.

At other times I have found myself able to fly around the house and on one occasion actually began to make my way to the Moon! We were house sitting for my Dad. It was morning time and Mick had just got up whilst I had a lie in! I suddenly felt myself going into a very relaxed state. So relaxed that I felt my body begin to seize up and become paralysed. This happens when I am either about to leave my body or I am coming back to it. My immediate reaction was one of fear but I quickly realised that there was nothing to fear. So I relaxed, went with it and got to a point where I could now exit my body... or so I thought. But it wasn't going to be that easy! Still paralysed, the spiritual me was trying to pull myself out, legs, arms even head first. But it wasn't happening. It was like I had a weight on top of me keeping me in. I knew this was just down to practice. However, when I relaxed I suddenly found myself outside of my body and floating above the bed. I realised that I could probably fly and so turned and headed for the bedroom window. I was in mid-air and now looking out of the window, a very strange sight had anyone been able to see it! I then turned and flew towards the bedroom door, out into the hallway and down the stairs. I got right up to the living room door when I suddenly had a thought. Having read up on out of body experience and astral projection I could now go anywhere I wanted, to a point, with a thought. The first place that came to mind was the moon! So I thought of the moon and then found myself flying through space towards the moon. It was taking a while but started to get very close. So close that the moon appeared so big to me that it was taking up my whole perimeter of vision. I couldn't see anything else, just pot holes and a yellowish white haze.

I couldn't believe it. I was doing this consciously; I was actually nearly at the moon. I then started feeling and hearing ringing in the ears of my physical body and decided that the moon, now that I was close to it, seemed pretty boring! I was happy with the progress I had made and so made the decision to go back to my body so I could get up and tell Mick all about it. I thought of my body and then felt myself falling back towards it. I made sure I didn't land with a bump and integrated back with my physical body smoothly. I then got up out of bed and told Mick everything who seemed hardly surprised anymore!

On another occasion in the early hours of the morning, whilst asleep in bed I suddenly felt myself falling. I seemed to be falling from a great height and all of a sudden my conscious mind took over and reminded me that this is what sometimes happens when I have been out of body. I realised that what would normally happen is I would land back in my body with a bump and so I decided to try and put the anchors on and slow myself down so I could land smoothly. I concentrated, my body still asleep but my consciousness very aware, and I started to consciously slow myself down. Just as I got near to landing back in my body I came almost to a standstill and then gently drifted like a feather back into my physical body. Then I physically woke up, felt a sense of achievement and went back to sleep!

You may have experienced awaking suddenly with a bump or a gasp. This can be due to you having been astrally projecting and being disturbed either in your astral body or your physical body, and your awareness is then suddenly being brought back to your Earthly body with a shock. It can be very quick and as you are pulled back to your physical body you almost come back with force, which is sometimes responsible for the bump.

Everyone astral travels every time they are asleep. The only thing is that most don't take conscious control during this time and so when they wake up they remember the events as a dream. In the dream state, when not in control, the dream can go from being relatively 'normal' to being completely bizarre. You can end up going further and further down a rabbit hole at which point it is safe to say that you are no longer having the dream, but the dream is having you. If you could become conscious during your dreams you could suddenly use this to your advantage and make each 'dream' a positive experience. Becoming consciously aware that you are in a dream is known as lucid dreaming and as stated, is another way in which astral projection can be achieved.

It is worth doing your homework if you plan to attempt astral projection consciously. There is much to know on this subject, such as how to ensure you are safe during your travels, how to achieve what you have set out to achieve and how to avoid becoming an energetic meal for those residing on the lower levels of the astral. One thing I always do when I find myself projecting is to imagine myself in a pure white impenetrable bubble that only those of the highest light and highest love can interact with. To imagine and feel this is to place that bubble of protection around yourself energetically and therefore it will remain with you on your travels. Use this also for your physical body and in your everyday life if you wish. We do this to ensure that our energy is as high as possible each and every day. You can also call upon the Angelic and other realms to help you when you are travelling in your astral body but always remember to state that any help must be from the highest light and the highest love and for your highest good, or words to that effect.

So having discussed astral projection and leaving the body physically whilst 'alive', what is the difference between having an out of body experience, and death? First of all it may help to know that each of us is connected energetically to our bodies by an etheric cord, an energetic link that allows us to experience life in the physical realm. This cord is a link from your soul self, the real you and is made of pure, pure love. When you are in an out of body state your etheric attachment is what keeps you connected to your body, it's like having a rope tied around your waist to find your way out of a cave. For some of those gifted with spiritual vision this etheric link has been described as a type of umbilical cord and as a rope made of pure light, a beautiful sight.

So then, the difference between an out of body experience and death is that upon death your etheric cord is severed preventing you from re-entering what was once your physical shell. This is the only way in which the cord can be disconnected from your body and it cannot happen just by being in an out of body state. There are those that have been on their deathbed and actually got as far as reaching the pearly gates only to be told at the entrance that they cannot enter. Suddenly they find themselves back in the room and very 'alive' having just literally died. So then how can that be? If they have died then their cord must surely have been severed? In these cases we believe it just isn't that person's time to go and divine intervention re-attaches them with their physical bodies allowing them to come back and tell the tail, if their cord was indeed detached at all.

I mentioned earlier about finding it difficult to slip out of the physical body. Mick made a very good and important point regarding this matter and about our etheric cords which was this; even though we are connected to our bodies by our etheric cords, if we could leave our body too easily it would be very dangerous. What would happen if we were one day crossing a road and we suddenly slipped out of our physical body? The answer is quite simple. You'd probably fall in front of a truck! So therefore there has to be some safety measures. Whoever created us knew that. So that's why, without practice it can be difficult to consciously leave our bodies. At least when projection occurs naturally when you are in bed, your body is safe and paralysis keeps it from thrashing around, preventing any injury.

Something amazing happened to us one night in 2010. We had just gone to bed and Mick had his arms around me. We both fell asleep fairly quickly in this position when all of a sudden I felt my sleep paralysis coming on. I couldn't stop it and had no choice but to go with it. All of a sudden I felt my crown chakra (energetic centre on top of the head), open, and a major rush of white energy started flowing in through my head and all through my body. I couldn't believe what was happening and was a little unsure at certain points so asked the Angels to be with me. I then had put into my mind the words "*Michael is with you*". I felt this was referring to Mick but knew all was okay then. Although I hadn't gone anywhere, I could feel that I was now occupying another level, albeit still within the confines of my physical body.

All of the time my whole being was vibrating and I could feel someone (or something) working energetically on my head and feel their fingers enter in through the back of my head and reach into my eye sockets. It sounds utterly bizarre but it actually felt very cleansing! Within my vision I was also being shown many images on a big screen as if being at the cinema. I felt these were to keep me calm and relaxed. One of the images involved a couple of puppies and the only other I remember was a vision of many pieces of fruit stacked in such a way it formed a beautiful picture. It was like watching a 3D film at the movies and a couple of times I even uttered the word "*wow*" in excitement. I made sure to ask for the energy to be used for the highest good and to be grounded into the Earth. Whilst this event seemed to be coming to an end I was aware that Mick had begun to snore and this had started to bring me around physically. I could see as he sat up in bed, looked above me for a couple of seconds and then look at me directly, looking very confused. He explained that he had just seen me hovering above where I was lying and that he couldn't actually see my physical body! I felt that he having his arms around me at this time was significant of protecting me as he is quite of that energy.

On another occasion, Mick and I stayed the night at my Mom's house. She had made the main bed up for us in her room and she slept in a downstairs bedroom with my young Niece. During the night, I didn't sleep too well and kept turning over. In the early hours of the morning, I turned over to see my Mom floating horizontally next to me, between the wardrobes and the bed! I was awake but dazed and thought nothing of this. She then spoke to me asking *"do you mind if I sleep here"*?! Still in a daze, I looked at her and replied "fine". I turned over again and this time went to sleep through till morning.

When I woke up, I remembered the event and was amazed. I couldn't believe that I'd seen my Mom *floating* next to me but not thinking anything unusual of it. I told her about it a short while later and asked her if she often flew around the house in an out of body state! She wasn't aware of this taking place but did remember being so uncomfortable sharing with my Niece and said that she had practically kicked her out of bed! Maybe her spirit self, decided she was going back to her own room!

The next story we wish to share is one that occurred only months before the writing of this book. It concerns transitioning into a parallel universe, completely by chance. This happened whilst we were home and our initial reaction was to call this event 'weird'. However we know now that what happened wasn't weird... it was in fact just another example of 'reality'. As I was on my way down the staircase into the living room, I saw Mick on the computer using a program similar to Ms

DOS, an old command prompt program that is nothing like the windows program we use today.

I thought nothing of this. Not until later when I thought to myself 'Mick wouldn't know how to use that program'! (No dis-respect to Mick) and if he ever found himself somehow on that program, I would definitely hear my name being called to fix it! So I asked Mick if he had been on this computer program to which he frowned and stated '*no*'. I explained what the program was and he confirmed one hundred percent that had he found himself on this kind of program, I would have known about it! But this felt and still feels like a 'real' memory, and not just that, it actually happened. So imagine our surprise when I next clicked on the desktop windows icon and found a program called 'command prompt' on the list of recently used programs. The exact kind of program I had seen on the screen earlier.

We forgot about this event for a few hours until it later popped back into the forefront of my mind. I had been looking through some information on the 'Indigo' generation of beings currently residing and incarnating on the Earth and some of the characteristics they possess. In between reading one particular essay on the subject, we began talking about the command prompt program incident! We concluded that I must have jumped into another dimension, an alternate reality be it however briefly. We have done this on a couple of occasions before and there just is no 'rational' explanation for it. We continued to read the article and received confirmation of what had been discussed in an amazingly synchronistic way. The article said "*...these people (Indigos) will have the ability to see the vast array of thoughts, dreams, wishes and needs of humanity, and to pop in and out of various dimensions at will to help work on these needs*". We knew then that a dimensional jump had occurred.

Scientists now accept and have even proven the existence of realities beyond our own. There will be a lot more information on this subject making it into the mainstream in the coming years as more and more people experience dimensions beyond their own and as more and more research adds credibility to these experiences.

Humanity has been programed to believe that this dimension (the third dimension) is the only existence when more and more evidence proves contrary to this. The very title of 'third dimension' suggests that there are dimensions before and after. Could it be, that this 'reality' is in actual fact also a 'dream' capable of being moulded to our needs and desires once one becomes conscious? It is a very real possibility. The problem is, having been fooled into believing this to be the only existence, the world has become very solid and less malleable than intended. We are capable of creating our own realities using the law of attraction and the power of manifestation, which we come onto later. We should be able to come and go from reality to reality, to visit our long lost loved ones, to visit planets even galaxies and beyond. There should be no limits, but we are limited by our belief systems that we are not worthy or that it is not possible. We have been duped into believing that what we have is all we are entitled to and no more, and because of this inherent belief which has been ingrained in us, we have attracted into our world that very way of being through the law of attraction.

Those behind the scenes, those that operate from the shadows of illusory control pray for you never to wake up. Because *when* you do, not *if* you do, humanity will discover once again what magnificent beings they really are, what they are capable of creating, not just for themselves but for each other. When this happens there will no longer be war in the world, there will no longer be starvation, famine, poverty or any other suffering of any kind, because everyone will have exactly what they need and we will all live and love as one.

We have been locked into this reality for far too long, through the constant feed of programming, negativity and suffering in our world.

Free your minds. It's time to break out of the cycle.

CHAPTER 5:

UFO's - Friends Or Foes?

Have you ever wondered why there are so many UFO sightings these days? With the increase of palm sized technology, footage is more easily captured and more widely available. But is this a coincidence or a deliberate act from beings of another existence to reveal themselves to us?

After Sarah and I met we became even more open minded than we were already, especially to the possibility of other life forms in our universe. Considering the size and vastness of it, it is not beyond the realms of possibility that humans are in fact not alone amongst the darkness of space, countless stars, planets and galaxies. Many researchers and scientists looking into this subject today tend to look for life as we know it; but what about life *as we don't know it*?

After a short while together as a couple, unexplainable things started to happen to us and we began to see a multitude of flying crafts that were quite obviously not orthodox. This was blatantly apparent to us by the manoeuvres and speed in which these craft moved and operated, and of course their trajectory path across the skies. Our sightings were so frequent that we became aware that a UK governmental department known as GCHQ had started monitoring our telephones and our computer activity and were taking an unusual interest in us. This was at a time that we were still police officers. We had seen large bright orange orbs (not Chinese lanterns), blue craft appearing from wormholes in the night sky, bright white objects that would just disappear in front of our eyes and even cigar shaped craft during the day. The sightings were amazing but we still didn't know why we were seeing them with such frequency. We did manage to get some photos of a couple of our sightings, which we included in our first book.

This period of our lives led us on a quest for answers. Answers to what these things were, who was on board them if anyone and why we were seeing them sometimes within days of each other. What we learned in the coming weeks and months shocked and excited us and had us thriving for more!

We discovered many things about why Earth is such a focal point at this time in our history given that we are going through so many changes and an awakening not seen since before many civilisations ago.

Everything is energy and energy is everything. Every thought that we think, every action we take and every deed we commit is an act of creation. Because our universe is connected, everything that we do has a ripple effect across the universe, so is it any wonder that other races of beings are showing an interest in what we are doing? Because the fact remains, what we do, affects them too.

Everything vibrates at a certain frequency and depending on the speed of that vibration depends on the density of the object in question. Humans vibrate very slowly and that is why we have the appearance of being solid. For us to see a UFO of a higher consciousness to ourselves and therefore vibrating quicker than us, that craft would have to slow down its vibrational speed in order for it to become visible in the available light accessible to us, within our physical sight and range. So therefore when you see a UFO of this kind, *they*, whoever they are, wanted to be seen. There are of course on occasions, mistakes made by lower density vessels and their occupants and as a result their cloaking technology will fail, allowing people to catch a brief glimpse of just what is actually above us. We have experienced this too in our home town. In the majority of cases it is a deliberate act of poking through into one dimension from another. Maybe this is all part of desensitising us and maybe it's a part of our awakening, a way of gentle introduction to the possibility of 'alien' life in an un-obtrusive kind of way. Whatever it is, it is happening and it is real!

It is safe to say that there are many forms of life different to our own. Some are not even physical but are etheric, not possessing physical bodies. Some are able to come and go from dimension to dimension and some are world famous. 'Alien' races such as the 'greys' depicted in many TV programs and Hollywood films are probably the most commonly known of them all. We've all read stories about the greys but what is their agenda? We believe that the intentions of some but not all of these beings as well as other alien races, are not of good will. The greys are an example of this fact as their intentions seem to be that of scientific and human genetic study, hence many stories of abductions of humans and also cattle mutilations. The mutilations are often performed with surgical precision and the animal's organs removed with not a trace of blood in sight. Studies have been conducted into this phenomenon with no 'rational' explanation having been concluded on. All of this is with a view to recreating artificial human emotion in order to assist in the longevity of their own race.

However the majority of other beings out there are from a good place and level of awareness and as Earth begins to rise in consciousness and vibration in readiness for the now famous year of 2012 and beyond, we have many races of cosmic beings working alongside us to assist. They are here both in their craft and on the ground. You may even be one of them, waiting for that 'go go go' command signalling the remembrance of your life's purpose and awakening you to your role here on Earth. So many people now are reporting buzzing sounds in their ears, sometimes diagnosed by medical professionals as Tinnitus. This in many cases, is informational downloads reaching out to our subconscious and that in turn is storing instructions for the near future so that at the flick of a switch we will automatically know what is required of us, what to do and where to go. This happens to us on a regular basis. Earth civilisations of the past have been reportedly awakened over night, when in reality they were probably being prepared by way of these informational downloads, triggers and keys so that when the time came, although it appeared that they had instantly awakened, they had been subconsciously ready for it.

There is an extra-terrestrial group of beings known as The Galactic Federation Of Light currently assisting us and headed by one known as Commander Ashtar on his lightship known to us as the 'Pegasus'. The Federation has many lightships above and around our planet at this time, tasked with different roles to assist us. So then is it any wonder that there are more and more sightings these days! This may all be sounding like something out of a Star Trek movie but these films aren't as fictional as you may think. Ideas such as these often have a factual base. Dr Spock for instance can be closely likened to a Pleiadian being, from the constellation of the Pleiades also known as the 'Seven Sisters'. This constellation can be seen in the night sky with the naked eye and it is well populated by many planets all at different levels of consciousness.

I have received many messages from Ashtar and the Galactic Federation of Light which we will come to in another chapter. The channelled messages are both encouraging and revealing. They lay claim to many of the sightings that we see in our skies and they have also stated that many of the crop circles that mysteriously appear across the world, particularly in rural Wiltshire of the UK, are in fact themselves communicating with us. We have both visited some of these formations and we can state without any doubt that they are far too complicated to be merely of Earthly origins. Sure there are those that are obviously hoaxed. These are apparent by the devastation caused to the crops and the rugged finish of the outlines. In contrast, the genuine formations show upmost respect for their canvas allowing the undamaged, interwoven crops to continue to grow back towards the sun within a couple of weeks so that they can still be harvested. There are many facets to these formations and there are many reasons for their presence. Some represent flags of various star nations, some represent the chakra points (energy centres of the body) and the spiralling energetic motions they take, others represent infinity and others are sacred geometric messages. Some emit informational energy into the Earth's atmosphere which connects on a subconscious level to our soul being and triggers much within us.

It is a known fact amongst many who study this phenomenon that these crop circles are actually complex messages brought to us in the form of sacred geometry and of course the universal language of mathematics. Everything has a sacred geometric shape; water, air, steam, ice, rain, everything you can think of when analysed closely enough. It is used widely at the point of creation and turns that which is un-manifest to that which is manifest.

With each new formation there comes more complexity in the messages that are left for us, languages not of our planet that as yet cannot be deciphered by the most advanced of Earthly computers. At the opposite end of the spectrum, there are also the most simplest of messages such as the famous humming bird formation which means 'infinity'. We know this because the humming bird is the only bird whose wings rotate in a figure of eight formation when flying and the numeral 8 means infinity, and that's what was meant by this formation. This is an attempt at communication from an intelligent source. The true magnificence of these formations can only be seen from the air. Shapes that appear circular, but are actually oval, made to look circular, is a difficult problem to address, but yet it has been addressed with such simplicity by an intelligent race.

Having visited these sites Sarah and I were amazed to see that the crops had been curved in many directions but not at all damaged. Flocks of birds have been known to break formation as they fly over a crop circle only to reform after they have passed over. They can sense the energy being emitted. This is truly the actions of cosmic intelligence and not the actions of humans in the darkness with a piece of wood, eluding the most sophisticated night cameras and the multitudes of watchers operating them. Instead it is mostly plasma balls of light forming them in a split second of creational genius. We are not saying that all crop circles are genuine. It is quite apparent that some are in fact hoaxes but these tend to be blatantly obvious as the area is a scene of devastation and destruction with crushed and broken crops without any consideration for nature and without the sophistication of interstellar messages. The genuine ones are just that, and are real. The crops are curved by an advanced knowledge of energy and gravity that release a warm static charge into our atmosphere, a good energy that you can sense and feel and know is helping mother Earth.

They are here, here to help us and teach us. Embrace our cosmic families as they embrace us and together we can move this planet forward. This is written in the growth of our Earthly crops for all of us to see and for the scientific community to decipher.

These beings of the cosmos, who many would call 'aliens' are actually our cosmic families and many of you may well be from the same planets of origin, having taken on a human form to accomplish certain aims. Many would have volunteered to come to Earth at this time to help with the consciousness awakening and ascension of both the planet and its inhabitants. Many of us have guides who are not of this planet, for example maybe from the Pleiades, Sirius, Orion, Neptune and other places. Sarah and I have a guide from Sirius who is part of the Galactic Federation of Light and due to the experiences that we have had and continue to have, we believe that we may be somehow connected to them too. So next time you see something in the sky that you cannot explain, say hello, you might be related! And they might just be looking back at you.

So Extra-terrestrials are amongst us, they have been a part of our existence on this planet since humankind first appeared as a race of beings. Much of our technology has been borrowed from an advanced source and many of our ancient monuments such as the Pyramids and Sphinx in Egypt were built with extra-terrestrial involvement. They walk amongst us, albeit sometimes on a different dimension.

We have heard so many times and have been asked even more *"Why don't they just appear, why don't they just give us a sign"*? Well they would say *"You show us a sign, show us a sign that you are ready for this greater truth"*. They do allow themselves to be seen but gradually so as to get mankind used to the idea of other existences and as we have already stated, due to the vibrational differences between us. It is not as simple as just appearing en masse; certain adjustments have to be made on both our parts in order for compatibility to occur. We know from personal experience that UFO's are tracked by the military and fired upon by jet airplane missiles. This is hardly a welcome gift from mankind to our family from the stars. And ask yourself, would you appear only to be met with such primitive converse? I doubt it! If you have long passed the need for war, the need for destruction, the backward thinking that creates this way of dealing with a problem, would you want to be dragged down into this chaos? We have to progress to a compatible level or least meet these beings of love half way for interaction to occur.

Sarah and I are mindful of the fact that we seem to be being built up for some kind of mass UFO sighting or visitation. We just recently and at the time of writing, read in a popular British newspaper an article stating that scientists suggest that we need to prepare for an alien meeting of some kind. We would urge everyone to just step back and use their intuition should this turn out to be the case. Be wary of false claims as our governments don't often make a habit of telling 'we the people', the truth! Your eyes and your minds can be tricked but not your intuition. It is your own internal defence mechanism, so our advice would be to work on it as much as possible and use it whenever the need arises. So if all of a sudden you were to see a large UFO, a ship from outer space, simply appear and present itself in a 'we come in peace' scenario, please consider this; would it be real? Are we as a whole, ready, vibrationally as well as emotionally? Until humankind is truly ready and has lifted its vibrations to that of a more equal frequency, and that is not just yet, we would ask you all to question it seriously if it is more than simply a UFO sighting, which are in the vast majority of cases genuine from both sides, that of the good guys and the bad.

There is a secret government development called 'Project Bluebeam' which in a nutshell is the technological capability to create a holographic image in the sky that appears real and solid, capable of fooling most in order to forward a particular view or agenda. It is also capable of putting ideas and thoughts into your psyche. If many researchers and that of inside information are correct, such a hoax is planned and the London 2012 Olympics have been linked with this. It is said that a large holographic UFO could appear in the skies over the Olympic stadium or close by, even in many countries simultaneously. This will give the impression that we are being visited or even invaded by extra-terrestrials. Of course, our governments also have access to physical UFO type vessels, back engineered over the years which would make such a spectacle all the more convincing. None of this may take place but it is best to be aware so we can make an informed decision if it does. It may be that we are able to prevent such a deception simply by enough of us being aware of it.

So why would someone want to deceive us to such an extent? Because if there is an apparent mass visitation/invasion from outside planet Earth then all nations of planet Earth would unite as one government, one global nation, and that's what those at the helm of all of this ultimately want, and how better way of getting it? On the face of it, this sounds like a good thing, but it isn't when the intentions of such aren't for the benefit of humanity. Those at the helm want a one world government ultimately for comprehensive control of all people and nations as in their occult belief systems they believe themselves to be the rightful rulers of a global planetary fiefdom. Project Bluebeam has many facets and this is just one of its purposes, we advise that you do your own research into this. The relevant information is easily available on the internet. You see if you study deeply enough, the agenda is spelt out for us in open fashion, not least by speeches given by various leaders. Remember the speech by the then American President Ronald Reagan in relation to the extra-terrestrial matter, who said referring to himself and the then Russian President Mikhail Gorbachev; "*...how easy his task and mine might be in these meetings that we held if suddenly there was a threat to this world from some other species from another planet outside in the universe. We'd forget all the little local* *differences that we have between our countries...*" implying that we would all come together to address such a threat. Therefore a staged alien invasion would likely bring about a one world government.

So what we call 'aliens' are already here with us and always have been in their various guises, captured for the benefit of history by cave drawings of ancient man and hieroglyphs in Egyptian times. However the more consciously advanced beings will only appear to us in a way that we are able to physically and emotionally handle; when we are truly ready. Otherwise it would cause us more harm than good and they wouldn't allow themselves to be a part of that. There are individuals that are ready for such contact but as a whole, we have a little more work to do to get there. However, it won't be as long as you may think...

They are here, they are with us, some of us are family to them, they will greet us and we them but only when the time is right. So, amongst the many races of 'life as we don't know it', we have many friends and of course just a few who we would not accept a party invite from.

Keep your eyes on the skies, and indeed all around you.

CHAPTER 6:

An Open Channel To The Stars

Channelling, what is it? I first began to channel telepathic messages from elsewhere at the start of 2010. At first it was fraught with difficulties and I could barely hear or feel the words presented to me. But over a period of time it got much easier and shortly after that I began to hear the words as if I was having a telephone conversation. It was quite apparent from the start that these words, sometimes accompanied with visual images, were not my own phrases or words at all. In fact they had a serious but hopeful message from many different beings of light. Sarah tends to channel in more of an artistic way and expresses this through her artwork.

I began to channel Archangels, Cosmic beings, Galactic Councils and many others. What was striking is that all of them basically gave a similar message of realism and yet hope and comfort. In this chapter I have listed some of my favourite channellings, which fit nicely into the theme of this book. Those channellings come from, Archangel Zadkiel, Michael, Raphael, Commander Ashtar and the Galactic Federation of Light, a cosmic group of many star nations here today to help the plight of humankind and planet Earth. Their messages were given to me so that I would be able to share them with as many people as possible and that's exactly what I intend to do.

A point to note here, is that there are many 'channellers' out there, all spreading information from various beings. So then, does that mean that everyone is channelling those from the light? Not necessarily. You see, as with anything in life you have to check the source of information and check that everything 'feels' right. I have worked on my intuition and continue to work on it to this day, even using the smallest of opportunities to develop it. It became apparent to us a short while ago that a lot of information out there was not coming from the right place and much information proved to be inaccurate, often leaving the recipients disheartened and disappointed. There is a lot of dis-information out there and many false messiahs so it is extremely important to exercise discernment and this will become more important in the coming days. Intuition is extremely important as it is your guiding star and will keep you on the path of truth when developed to a high level.

Having said this, there are also a number of genuine sources out there, you just have to look a little harder to find them! But they are there and the messages and information they give will resonate within your heart as you will know them to be true.

An easy rule that we follow is this; if it doesn't feel right then let it go! We all have the ability to access the wealth of universal knowledge and communicate with higher vibrational beings, it just takes practice and a strict intuition.

Archangel Zadkiel:

"The human race is unstoppable when you act as one, when you walk along the same line together, when you speak as one voice. You are more powerful than you could ever realise dear ones, more powerful than you often care to realise. Then why do you not join forces and turn around the world upon which you live. Remove the chains of slavery that don't belong around your necks.

You allow your power to be held by others and not you, take it back and do good things for each other, we will help you, just ask, but take back what is yours, that being in control of your own lives. Your life is your unique experience, live it, it belongs to you and no one else. You have given it away in many cases, given your power away to your leaders, your authority figures and many others who do not have the right to control you and enslave you.

Stand up for yourselves, stand up for what you believe in and exercise love as a means of communication to others. You are free, you are infinite consciousness, reclaim your brilliance, it is yours, find it and be it, you are worthy and capable of using it for only good.

Believe me when I say it is there, it may be hidden in many of you but it is there within you. Look inside yourselves and find it. Express your magnificence and live your endless possibilities, that is you, the real you, how you are and always will be. When you know what you really are you remove any limits imposed upon you, either by you or those who don't know you.

Be free my friends, be forever free, I am Zadkiel".

Archangel Zadkiel:

"*Live each day, enjoy each day, embrace each day and do all that you can to find ultimate pleasure and happiness each day. Now is all that is important, now is your past, present and future combined, tomorrow is your future but it will be still the now, it shall be the now but then. Take each day as it comes and live and do all that you can, enjoy your life and do the things that you like to do. The systems that enslave you will break down eventually, things just got worse unexpectedly, this wasn't how things were meant to be, it is how they turned out, much to our dismay. Now we must act to reverse this trend for the sake of all upon your planet. Now is a good time to start, much has already been done, and much is still to be done, and it shall be.*

Mankind is finally waking up to a better way, one that is not slavery, one that brings paradise to you. Once you realise and acknowledge that there is a better way then you can bring it into being. You are doing this, wake up as many others as you can and we can then bring this about much faster, Thank you, I am Zadkiel".

Archangel Zadkiel:

"Time, another illusion contained within your realm. Beyond your realm time has no relevance, it is a fabrication of the mind, and it is your master. When we say to you your desires are around the corner to us that is what we mean, to you it means now, instantly. Imagine a place where time does not exist, that is our quandary. We don't exist by these rules, be patient when we forecast good things for you, they do arrive at a time they are meant to be. There is such a difference between your realm and ours, the one we occupy in the heavens, and we may sometimes enter to help you or make contact with you but then we return and go back to our own environment, it is where we are comfortable.

You need to lift yourselves vibrationally so that you too can join us there and we can become one once again. After your experiences there on Earth you will return to us, many will do it before your time there is up. This is a wonderful proposition and those ones will be most welcome. I will leave you now dear ones, but I will be back soon, I am Zadkiel".

Archangel Zadkiel:

"Special moments become longer than just a moment, knowledge becomes more than just knowledge it becomes your life. When you

walk the path of enlightenment your life changes, you feel every day is a special moment for you and everyone else and you become free, you take back your life and you call your own shots.

Rely on only you and you will always be happy with the result, you don't need to rely on others for anything. That only serves in giving your power away. Be self-sufficient and be self-fulfilled. You are your own power, you are in control of your own life, don't allow others to judge you or rule you, they do not have that right, that would be a mark that they cannot step over.

Take back your power, it was given to you, if only you knew how magnificent you were you would never seek another's permission ever again. That is you, the real you, remember who you are my friends, you will be amazed at what you will find. I am Zadkiel".

Archangel Michael:

"*Be grateful for yourself and be at one with your soul, after all that is the real and true important you. Many have fallen at this first hurdle because they have not listened or even acknowledged their own inner guidance and their own inner knowledge. This is your truth, this is an open channel of communication from which we talk to you dear ones. Always use discernment but open up yourselves and open up your channels and be ready to receive much more from a higher place, the place in which your true you resides.*

Speak from your heart and speak with only pure love for others. You may come from a position of knowing this but they compared to many of those from the light are still in the dark ages. Be patient with them and let them catch up in their own time, they are not all at the same level or stage of development as you. If you can see this and understand this then conflict will be resigned to a thing of the past. Be mindful of how you react to any given situation and in turn the situation will be mindful of how it reacts to you. You know all this but there are many who do not and this is me reaching out to them. We need many ways in which to have our voices heard. We find a way amongst many who are ready to take this important role on and we thank you. We are grateful to you for without you we would in many cases have been silenced in the vibrations of your realm. I hope that many will hear my messages and that they bring hope and a true sense of reality for you.

I send you my Love, my protection and my infinite guidance. Thank you all, my love is yours to feel. I am Michael".

Archangel Michael:

"Sometimes you feel that you have veered off your path. Sometimes you think that all is lost when it isn't. It is just change, that what you once used to resonate with has gone, the people who you used to call your friends are no longer seen as such. You have, putting it simply, moved on. Your old memories are a past that you no longer look at with the same fondness. The new you cannot be held back by the old you and as you move forward with quickening pace then the past will become more and more distant to you. Go with it, don't fight it, new ventures, new friends, new opportunities and new beginnings surely await you.

It takes great courage to do this, it takes great strength to move on into new ground, it is not always the easiest route, a path of least resistance, it is hard and sometimes difficult and we only choose the strongest souls to take on this often seemingly thankless task. Be uplifted by the fact that you were chosen, like those who you have come into contact with at this time for a dual purpose, they too were chosen.

From this day on and from this day forward you will come into contact with the people who you need in your life, to move forward together, many who you once resonated with have stopped buzzing. Keep to your own divine purpose and stay focussed on that path to your own destiny. Your dreams await your arrival. Have faith and be at peace. Sometimes you create your own chains to tie you down, release yourself and be free. Don't take the strains that you don't need to. A journey that holds pleasure and relative ease is the path of choice, the path you need to walk along. Any other path that feels rocky and full of effort is the wrong route. Be gentle on your feet and take a journey that is forever smooth, you already know this to be a true fact. We know those who commit themselves to divine service and we are sent to nurture them, you grow like the most beautiful of gardens and you shine brighter than the brightest star, we know you and we are with you offering our help, support and guidance. We ask that you accept it and take it from us and as for the ones who do not yet see, we are working on them!

Thank you all once again. I am Michael, God's protector".

Archangel Michael:

"Don't let worry get the better of you, don't let illusion stifle you, it is but only a mist that you call your reality. It is a self-inflicted outcome that you impose onto yourself. Look beyond that illusion, look beyond that mist, it is only a temporary reality for you, not at all what is the real you. This is an experience for you, don't get involved with unnecessary complications, there is no need to get bogged down with

lower energy illusion, remain the real magnificent you, remain at your own high levels of existence and don't come tumbling down because of the opinions and actions of others. This is your experience, let them have their own and don't allow them to influence you and take away your focus. Many will try, resist it and move on. Now you are at this stage, you know what you must do, you are in a good place, the right place for you, everyone is in the right place for them, you will all reach your destination but at different times, sometimes different lives.

Many of you have been on Earth and indeed on other realms and planets many times, that was your chosen evolutionary path, the path your soul chose to learn and experience physicality. Just know that there is more to existence than the existence you live in at the present moment, so much more. You are all consciousness and you are infinite creation, now do you still need to worry? No you do not. Live your life with joy and childlike excitement, that is how it was meant to be, heavy lower energies are bad and will not be around forever, this is towards the end of its cycle, be uplifted by this fact. Things are changing for you, things are getting better for you all, you will be aware of this fact in due course when certain things have run their course, of that be assured.

I love you all my warriors of Light, I am always with you. I am Michael".

Archangel Michael:

"Hello to you all again. Today is a good day, today is important in the sense that it is where you are in your development, today is your peak, every other day has led you up to now. Take what you can from this day before you move on to tomorrow. In other words now is all you should be thinking about, don't worry about the future, it has not yet happened, live for the now, for that is where you occupy. Take one day

at a time and master that, take all that you can from that time. Too many of you worry about things that may not even happen, worry is not good for you, be at peace and let things take care of themselves for once. Love your life, it is an experience like no other, when you return to the higher realms it would have bode you well in your teachings of others. Enjoy your time there on Earth, you have an eternity to be elsewhere. Thank you and enjoy your day, I am Michael".

Archangel Michael:

"In recent days I have spoken much about the darkness, but let's detract from them, their grip is loosening. In the coming days they will be no more and all can move on with your reality. I was sent by the creator to oversee events on Earth and I do just that, I view these things from a better position and can see the overall picture. Your future looks good for the many who concentrate on the divine. Those who are not with us yet must be soon so as not to miss out on what is rightly yours and what is achievable. Come with me and follow the wishes of the divine creator when I say things will change for you all at a time that is soon.

2012 is mentioned widely amongst your race, you needn't be concerned with what might or might not happen, just be concerned with you and where you are when the time comes. Only you can do this and place yourself in the right place for you. It is so important that this be the case, for the time is near, are you ready? Only you know the answer to that question, deep down you know the truth about your current situation. Be part of the exodus of light, when we make our move, be with me. I am Michael. I am your protector".

Archangel Michael:

"Times like these are rare, times when things don't make much sense are here, you are living in them. More and more of you are asking why, asking the questions and demanding an answer.

Continue on that path and expect your answers, don't accept anything less. So many questions need answering, so many of your leaders refuse to acknowledge the answers you seek. You must keep up the pressure on them to be truthful for this is not their usual state and they feel uncomfortable trying to tell you the true reality. A place of dishonesty is where they reside, where they feel safe and secure, their demons reside there with them. They too do not always see just what it is they do, the system they champion, it must be pointed out to them in the hope that they will change just as many of you have already changed for the better.

Show them your love and be pitiful to them because they chose the wrong path and it is for them to alter their course from the one of power, control and self-indulgence. Your world is changing, hold onto your well founded beliefs that this is the case.

I leave you now with this fact; Heaven will soon be upon your wonderful Earth, get yourselves ready and be wholly prepared dear ones.

I send you my love and my gratitude. I am Michael".

Archangel Raphael:

"I am Raphael and I am the Angel of healing. Your world endures many poisons in the food that you eat and the water that you drink. You

should be careful as to what you place inside your vessels, they need to remain pure for optimum health. It is not too late to change your ways, it just takes a little thought to gain a better understanding of how things are for you all.

Eat well, but be conscious of what it is you digest, your wellbeing depends on it. Stay healthy and pure so that you may become enlightened once again, I ask that these things happen. Call upon me for guidance in these matters. I am Raphael and I am the Angel of healing and health".

Mother Mary:

"*Beloved ones, your Earth is going through a time of transition and is raising her vibrations and you must too in order to go with her into the higher realms of consciousness. Take from this the experience that you need and go with her. Don't be left behind when the time comes for this change, your Earth cannot wait much longer, she is in pain and in need of love. Do what you can to appease her loneliness. Thank you, Mother Mary*".

Galactic Federation of Light:

"*More and more of you are believing it can be done, more and more of you are gaining in hope, you have a right to be, you are getting there. It was a concern for us in the past that things had gone too far and that it may have been too late but that is no longer the case, you deserve some credit for that fact. Because of the efforts of many your world has a chance and is beginning to turn herself around. It is still not plain sailing we have lots to do, but we have the opportunity now of that chance. Concentrate on what it is you must do in the coming days of your history and prepare for that day. Many of you have already had the calling and know what it is you must do, many of you will just know when the time comes and it is right. Either way your roles have been set and will be activated within you all. Many have agreed to help this cause at this time, now is that time, be ready to take up your positions for the final charge. That is all for now. Thank you and take care. We are the Galactic Federation of Light".*

Galactic Federation of Light:

"Dear beloved people of Earth, many of you are waking up, many of you are shinning your divine light that much more brightly. It is making the difference and having much impact on your world. We ask that you continue to do just this and make the final push for light and banish the dark forever. You are doing well and you are getting there, you are nearer than you realise, we can see this happening, we can see all from our position above your planet and of course from our people on the ground. We remain here until your planet comes into alignment with all others in terms of synchronicity and ways. What you do affects all our universe and beyond and we all have an interest in your affairs. We are here to help you, we are here to help planet Earth, she too is alive and has needs, be gentle and kind to her and she will repay her debt to you for taking such action. Let her suffer no more like she has previously. One day we shall all be united in a common cause and your planet will again be in alignment and a complete part of the synchronicity of the whole universe once again. Thank you and God bless. We are the Galactic Federation of Light".

Commander Ashtar (Galactic Federation of Light):

"I am Commander Ashtar, my ships circle your Earth and are responsible for many of your sightings, but not all, some of them do not come from a good place but I will deal with those. Don't be too concerned with them. We have come en masse by divine authority with many races of beings at this time in your history to help you. We have travelled from many star systems and galaxies to be with you now at this time. We are needed by you as things have got out of hand, stating the obvious. We circle your planet waiting for the time in which to act, waiting for you to ask us for help. That day should be soon, we have travelled far for you. You are all part of the universe and therefore you are a big part of us, and we you. We have come back to see many of you again as you are our families from our own planets. Little do you know about your origins, they would amaze you.

We should be asking you for stewardship such is your potential but until you have sorted yourselves out that is not the case...yet, I wish to add. Check out the information you receive and use your discernment when you come across beings claiming to be ourselves, we are the Galactic Federation of Light and we are truth and love, you will know within your hearts who is real and who is not, any doubt that you may have is your own defence mechanisms in place. We hope to be working with you all soon when the time is right for all of us.

Until that day my friends I am Ashtar".

Sarah's depiction of the Galactic beings assisting us on Planet Earth

Galactic Federation of Light:

"Hello people of Earth, there will be an increase in sightings in the coming months, very few of them will be publicised, many of them will not be us but they will happen nevertheless. Your governments are desperate to withhold the truth, they fear enlightenment in any form and they will stop at nothing to keep it away from you the people.

They shall not succeed, the truth is much more powerful than their lies. Don't be afraid when you see things in the sky that you cannot explain, see what you feel in your heart before you decide its origins.

You will know when you see a ship of the light for that's how it shall appear to you. If it doesn't then it isn't. Be wary of false sightings and false explanations, we do exist, we are with you and amongst you but so are those who don't come from a place of love.

We can deal with those and we will when the time comes. Although we are peaceful we do have capabilities that far exceed any technology you would have seen or experienced and we come with divine authority to act on your behalf.

You must do your part, Earth was a gift for you and you must defend your planet. We again thank you and we hold you in high esteem, you have been away for a long time and we look forward to being reunited with you after our work is done.

We have missed our families. Go and save your beautiful Earth and then return home those of you who belong elsewhere. Until we communicate with you again take care and look to the stars and say hello, we can hear you, we are the Galactic Federation of Light".

Galactic Federation of Light:

"We do not come to rescue you, we come to help you to rescue yourselves. You must take the helm and you must take the lead to solve the problems that are ever present on your beautiful planet and indeed your everyday lives.

Wake up and see that you are being forced into servitude, forced to be slaves to a system designed to make you a slave. You are more than that but you have to realise just how much more you are before anything can begin to change.

It must change and it must be made to change, it is your planet and it is your future at stake. Do you not want more for yourselves, do you not think that as a race you are better than what you are taught to expect, which falls far short of what you should have.

You are magnificent beings and as soon as you realise this you will return to this state of being. Be the fantastic race that you are and be the love that your planet needs right now. No more can Earth be treated like this, disasters every day the likes of which have not been seen for a long time.

Your authorities do not tell you the full extent of the damage caused and they will not, they fear the public outcry and reaction and they have no answers to your questions, they have no cures for the ills they create and allow to happen and they have no will to stop a re-occurrence.

There is a better way and it shall come in the not too distant future, it is time to start again, start anew and live how it was intended, with love, respect, honour and integrity, everyone as part of the whole universe and all part of the oneness.

Paradise on Earth and it is coming dear ones, it is coming soon. We thank you all for accepting our words, we are the Galactic Federation of Light".

Galactic Federation of Light:

"Your role models are not worthy of this accolade, the ones you entrust are not trust worthy. Don't worship figures of fame just because they have fortune. Many of these figures are shallow and live their own dream not worrying about the ones who have nothing. This is an imbalance that cannot continue if you are to move forward, you are all

equal, you all start as a spark of creation on equal terms, you remain on those equal terms.

Greed and apathy cause this imbalance, the material desire for more even when you have more than enough, more than you could ever need. Rise above this dear ones and love your Earth and love your fellow man and see that you all have sufficient things to enjoy your experience on Earth.

When you see and feel beyond the illusion of material wealth you realise that love is the greatest wealth of all, it is priceless. Be grateful and be appreciative of the beauty and the wonders that you see and be happy that you are able to see them, that is a true gift as you see the evidence of creation.

We remain above your planet Earth sending our energy and our love to you, you may well feel it, you may just know that it is there. When you look up at the night sky you sometimes see home, that is where many of you originate from and you shall one day return to your home planets to be reunited with your families.

You have all done well and have experienced lots in the time you have spent on Earth. You will use that knowledge to good effect when you get back home. For now you must help planet Earth, that is your goal and you volunteered to do this, in fact you were in many cases insistent. This is the sign of a strong soul and a hardy spirit. You have shown this with each new challenge you face, with each new difficult decision you make, well done.

You will make it and we will help you, together we unite for the good of many and we love you all, we are your family, the Galactic Federation of Light".

Galactic Federation of Light:

"Galactic Federation of Light, many of you know exactly who and what that is, many of you know that we are a coalition of star nations with many races of beings sent to Earth to help with the ascension of humankind.

We are here, we have travelled across many galaxies to be with you at this time in your history, some of us are from places you have heard of, places that you can see with your own eyes. Whatever the case may be we are here in your skies and upon your planet. Many of you are our foot troops even though you don't realise it yet. You will know your role when you are called upon, you will know what to do.

With such help focused upon your planet right now you can get a sense of how important a job this is, the ascension of Earth and indeed yourselves is a major issue for many of those who are here to help you. We are your friends and we are your family and we want to see you succeed. Give a little thought and a little time to review just why you are here now at this time of great importance for you all.

That may wake many of the dormant helpers up and become activated once again. You all need to wake up to the fact that you are unlimited possibility who are not to be controlled or enslaved by anyone, free yourselves and be what you really are.

Do you think that you were created to work until you die, struggle to afford to eat, have nothing and be satisfied with scarcity, you were not. You were created out of love to enjoy life and to have plenty, to learn and experience beauty and to have joy and fun.

That shall be returned to you, demand all that is yours, that is your right and don't accept anything less my friends, you are deserving of all things. Take care dear ones and please consider all that we have said to you.

Until we next communicate with you be yourselves and be great, you are a wonderful creation of light. Farewell dear ones, in Love and Light".

Galactic Federation of Light:

"Hello people of Earth. It has been many days of your time since we spoke last. A lot has happened in that relatively short space of your Earthly time. You can now begin to see the changes and indeed feel the changes upon your planet and within yourselves.

Take stock of what you can see and sense, for it is real and you are transcending into your new reality. It may seem strange and it may feel *uncomfortable but you will adapt as you always do, you are hardy and can blend into your new surroundings. There is much to be pleased about, there is much goodness to delight upon. You are raising yourselves accordingly to the grand divine plan. We take great comfort in seeing this from the vantage point of your skies, it is a wonderful sight to behold.*

It gives us great pleasure to see you becoming a part of the 'All That Is'. We are all 'One' and we must act as if we are all 'One', that is the only state of being that is real, all else is illusionary. You are beginning to realise that you are more than this, you are starting to question your own purpose and know that you have much more to give.

Continue on this path of awakening dear ones for it is leading you to the right place, the route is mapped out for you all by us. Just follow the signs, follow the cats-eyes that illuminate your way and keep walking towards our open arms.

God bless you all, we are proud of you all".

The Galactic Council:

"Twists and curls of genetic strands that give you the picture of the essence of life, the essence of existence. Strands of light that cross and separate, glow and dissolve.

A universe that spirals with cosmic energy, the gift of knowledge, the gift of just knowing that you can access that knowledge. Sparks of light that become existence, a being, a member of our cosmos, each a part of all and nothing going to waste.

Each a valued form and each a valued aspect of my love and your love. Isn't this wonderful? Isn't it beautiful to know? I know and you know and we all know and we all want to know, for these secrets belong to all of us.

We are all one being, we are all one consciousness, we are all one and we will all remember that we are all one now and forever in our rightful state of eternity.

We are the Galactic Council and we share our thoughts with you all, for the day of oneness is rapidly approaching you dear ones, it shall be here with you soon and we will be with you soon".

So it is encouraging that we have so much help and assistance at this time in Earth's history. We have highlighted just some of the messages that have been telepathically received over a relatively short period of time. Although some are either from Archangels, Galactic beings or Galactic councils, all are evidentially working together as one to achieve a universal goal and that goal is the betterment of humankind and planet Earth.

Let's be grateful and help them to help us.

CHAPTER 7:

The Ancient Wonders Of Egypt - The Truth

When you mention Egypt to anyone it is almost a certainty that they would immediately think of the Great Pyramids of Giza and of course the Sphinx. These monuments are world famous wonders that are visited by all nationalities each and every day of each and every year. Talk to Egyptologists and alike and they will tell you that slaves built these structures over a 20 year period and that they were used for ancient burials for the Kings and Pharaohs of Egypt.

But what if this is incorrect and these structures had a very different purpose, one that is not widely known or recognised in today's mainstream teachings? What you will read in this chapter will probably change the way in which you view these ancient wonders and may challenge what you have been taught throughout your life. It certainly did us.

We aim to explain how what was intended to be our annual holiday actually turned out to be a voyage of discovery for us, unlocking many secrets of the ancient world and part of the history of planet Earth. It had been pre-arranged from above for this journey to have been possible.

Over the last several years Sarah and I have had many spiritual experiences and as a result of these we have become what has been described as 'Lightworkers' and we are striving to expand our consciousness into the higher realms and become complete and fulfilled beings. Because we are a team who have incarnated on the Earth at this particular time in her history our light is more potent and these occurrences for us are more focused and powerful and quite obviously pre-ordained.

In January 2010 Sarah and I began to get a strong sensation that we needed to go to Egypt. We were incidentally looking for a location in which to go on holiday anyhow but we knew that this was more than just a simple vacation, it was a longing that just didn't disappear. Some of our spiritual friends had the same feeling but their calling was to different parts of the globe, such as India. It seemed as though a much larger picture was forming and when divine service calls you the only solution is to act upon the call and go with the flow to fulfil that calling... wherever it takes you!

So this story for us in any case begins here and we looked for many days until we found just the right place to stay in Sharm El Sheikh, Sinai. Our trips were pre-booked including a visit to Giza, the home of the great Pyramids and the Sphinx. From that point on things began to unfurl and everything appeared to be preparing us for the trip. Both Sarah and I had strong intuitive feelings that this was far more than just a holiday. The holiday was a facade and a means of getting us there. We could sense that we had significant work to do once we arrived there. This was exciting for us and we were ready and waiting for whatever was awaiting us both.

In the days that followed I received a phone call from a local Reiki Master who we had known for some time. She told me that she was getting a message that there was a book at her spiritual centre that both Sarah and I needed to read. After the conversation had ended I thought nothing more of this book and it didn't arise again for some time. Several weeks later she called me again, this time regarding a completely separate non related issue and at the end of this conversation out of the blue she again mentioned that there was a book at the Centre that she felt strongly we needed to read. She couldn't remember the exact name or subject matter only that it would be of interest to us and that it mentioned aliens! She gave us a general location as to where we could find it.

Sarah went looking for the book, as we knew that to have had this mentioned twice was a sign for us to act upon it. Sarah didn't have any trouble locating the book. We took the book home with us not knowing why we needed to read it. The cover had pictures of crop circles and aliens, which are subjects that we are both very interested in, but other than that it seemed to have no relevance to our venture. We didn't look at the book again, not even a peek inside but instead we packed it into our suitcase deciding to read it in Egypt, and not before.

It didn't end there. Again out of the blue we received an email from a Reiki Master who lived in Scotland who had found us through our own website. We began emailing each other but at no point did I mention Egypt to her. This was one of the first emails that we received from her:

"Michael and Sarah,

You will both help to uncover more insights and translate ancient knowledge brought to us from great distance. Your decisions in travel over the next few years will determine how and when you begin the next phase. Good Luck!.."

At that point I told her that we had booked a trip to Egypt for February 2010 and then we received this email from her:

"... All I will say is, you're in the right part of the world. If you are able to, there is something for you at the feet of the Sphinx. You will need to tune in to receive it though. Don't worry if you can't get close, a messenger will find you..."

We knew that we would be emanating our light into what is ordinarily a dark place in energetic terms, and that our trip was to be a working holiday so to speak. The final email we received regarding Egypt came just before we left for the trip itself and detailed a message that this individual herself had received from above regarding our trip. This is the final message:

"... About the darkness, your light is needed and your job will be tough at times, but you have each other for grounding and protection. Your own energies will be transformed. As long as you look past the tourism and see Egypt for what she really is. Work with her energy. I understand your message to be - 'Under the Sphinx lies an ancient secret knowledge that will be added to your toolbox. Use this wisely and for the benefit of ALL. All meaning past, present and future. It all belongs together, in the same place. You must absorb, accept, understand and finally KNOW. Only then can you share and teach..."

This information had been given to her by her own divine 'board of directors'. She had been their interpreting channel and had subsequently passed the information on to ourselves. It was very much valued and appreciated. Although Sarah and I didn't know the identity of the board, such information tends to reach the person or persons it was intended to reach, and this information was of great importance to us and our venture. Well by now many pieces had just fallen neatly together for us both and we could sense that higher forces were near and working with us. We have learned that when things fall so easily into place then it is meant to be, and this trip ticked all of those 'meant to be boxes'!

So we arrived in Egypt using the first couple of days to acclimatise to the heat and the surroundings and it was then that over a period of several evenings Sarah began to pick up the book that we had borrowed. To our complete amazement many chapters were about Egypt and its connections to Atlantis. As I mentioned previously there were no clues to this on the book cover it was only when we started to read it that it became clear. I suppose you can't judge a book by its cover! Although we didn't know it at the time this book turned out to be the messenger that we had been told to expect. We had assumed that the messenger would have arrived in either human or spirit form but we were wrong.

Giza was the first excursion of our holiday. That just seemed right and we took an internal flight to Cairo. We had a full day in Cairo visiting the museum and alike saving the main event, the Pyramids and the Sphinx until last. Again this seemed the right way of doing things. Our expectations had been left to build and grow along with our excitement throughout the day.

As we arrived at the Pyramids both Sarah and I looked at them with a sense of familiarity. We had expected to be in awe of these wonders but we had a feeling that we had been here before. We had been told a long time ago that we had both been together in ancient Egypt and Atlantis in past lives. Although all three Pyramids were magnificent in size, workmanship and structure, for me I had a deep and strange feeling and sensation about the centre Pyramid. This was causing me to vibrate from head to toe, as if I had a mild electric current flowing constantly through me. My stomach was much the same and was turning over and over like a washing machine. There was something special about this centre Pyramid more so than any of the others which gave me hardly any reaction at all.

We spent a few hours at the Pyramids soaking up the marvel of the surroundings, trying to imagine how they would have looked in those days of old, coated in the splendour of white marble with a Golden point at the top. It was now time to make our way towards the Sphinx which was a short travel away from the Pyramids. As we arrived at the next location we were shepherded into a small contained concrete type structured building out of sight of the great Sphinx. The area was so crowded that movement was restricted and sight was obscured. Eventually it was our turn to move along a narrow passageway uphill towards where the Sphinx was situated. This structure was still out of sight, but as I moved ever closer I again began to constantly vibrate all over and again my stomach began to turn, although these sensations were not unpleasant something was happening to me on a much deeper level than the physical. It was a strange feeling and my senses were being stirred.

As we reached the top of the uphill slope I looked to my right and saw the Sphinx in all its size and true glory. Although the area was crowded with tourists, Sarah and I included, as I walked to the closest place we could get to the Sphinx, a gap large enough for two people (myself and Sarah) appeared in front of us! Again this was perfectly timed and as far as we were concerned, pre-arranged and not coincidental. Incidentally we found ourselves in perfect alignment with the right paw/right neckline and head of the Sphinx so that we were looking directly at it from the right hand side.

As I stood with the chaos behind me and around me, I closed my eyes briefly to try and tune in to whatever it was I needed to see. Thousands of years of history stood with me and almost immediately in my third eye (psychic eye) I was shown a structure that I can only describe as some sort of dimensional gate to other dimensions and other realms.

The machine was not ugly to the eye it was advanced and simple looking. This dimensional gate was directly in line with where we were standing, in direct alignment with the Sphinx's right side from head to paw and beyond.

I was also shown that this machine or structure goes underground and connects to the centre Pyramid deep below the surface of the desert sand and obviously out of sight. This is why I had such a strong reaction to the centre Pyramid, but not any of the others. Both the Sphinx and the centre Pyramid were deeply connected with underground passageways and dimensional gates connecting them both together. The constellation of Orion and more specifically Orion's belt is significant also. The top of the centre Pyramid is directly aligned with the centre star of Orion's belt and when the two are perfectly aligned energetic grids are activated. The centre star of Orion's belt is also a star gate and completes the circuitry between the dimensional doorways of these grandiose structures and the universe.

When you learn to listen to your intuition you learn to acknowledge that what you are receiving in the form of messages from higher realms is true, and this information was very true and changes the way we see these wonders, which we will get to later.

It seemed as though when we had been given this information in a visual and physical sense, we would come across the same information sometime after in the book we had borrowed as exact confirmation. What we have also learned about these structures is also very interesting and bares no resemblance to what mainstream education would have you believe.

This all started in Earth's ancient past. Many millenniums ago there was a Luciferian rebellion (Lucifer is known in many religions as the name of the devil). Lucifer was a fallen Archangel who wanted to be better than the being some refer to as 'God'. He convinced a large number of followers, who we know as fallen Angels to join forces with him and he recruited them to work with him. He wanted to be able to perform the divine feats of 'God' without using the love element, thereby creating without 'God' who creates everything from the heart, with love; a sort of artificial creation.

Lucifer created what is known as an external merkaba so that he could create things externally rather than from within, from the heart. By doing things this way you shut yourself off from 'God' and the light and therefore, love. Also by doing things this way you become reliant upon the technology created to do things for you and you begin to shut yourself off from a lot of your own natural abilities to create and manifest.

Merkaba, also spelled merkabah, is the divine light vehicle used by Ascended Masters and higher beings to connect with and reach those in tune with the higher realms. 'Mer' means light. 'Ka' means spirit. 'Ba' means body. Mer-Ka-Ba means the spirit/body surrounded by counter-rotating fields of light, (wheels within wheels), spirals of energy as in DNA, which transports spirit/body from one dimension to another. It is a vehicle of divine creation.

A group from ancient Mars, known as the Martians were part of this Luciferian rebellion and as a result of this their own planet became messed up and they needed to find an alternative planet upon which to reside. You guessed it... Earth, (and how lucky we all are)!

Using the external merkaba that they had created they managed to create a time space vehicle (what we know today as a UFO), and with it they found Atlantis here on Earth. Atlantis was a thriving peaceful and loving society at that time. Because the Martians were technologically advanced they believed that they would be able to take over Atlantis but because they didn't have sufficient numbers to do this, they failed and had to live the way of the Atlantians, albeit very reluctantly.

The Martians had to try and live with emotions and love in order to fit in with society, which they actually and surprisingly managed to do for a very long time. But eventually this wasn't to their desires and they again tried to take over, only this time they somehow managed to cause a dimensional tear which allowed and enabled numerous spirits and other entities, that didn't belong on this dimension, to pass through and cause havoc.

By this time, a seed had been planted and a large number of Atlantians had been converted to the technological, external ways of the Martians. Sometime in the history of the latter days of Atlantis it was discovered that a huge asteroid was headed towards the Earth, in particular where the Martians resided. Although many of the great Masters of Atlantis were able to stop this happening, they wouldn't because in their eyes and the eyes of the unconverted Atlantians; 'what will be will be'. They believed everything to be in divine order. The Martians eventually decided to leave, but they left behind them a destructive legacy and enough people who were willing to rely on left sided brain technology, as they had. This amongst other things, including the darker side of people's egos, eventually caused the downfall of Atlantis and with it, the 'Golden age'. The dark forces simply took hold, seeking a machine existence rather than one based on divine manifestation and love, as the source or 'God' had intended.

The Masters of the day attempted to cause a synthetic planetary Christ consciousness to heal the situation but it had gone too far. Some of the

Masters and former leaders of Atlantis, held the blue print for the grid of Christ consciousness and they took it with them to the place we know today as Giza, in Egypt. By doing this they believed that all would reach a state of expanded consciousness and be able to solve the problems together, in love.

This was the chosen location because it was one of Earth's axis points and the collective consciousness was able to emerge there. The Great Pyramids of Giza were then built or at least influenced by them over a period of three days, with extra-terrestrial involvement, with a sole purpose of changing human DNA and consciousness to that of Christ consciousness and enlightened beings. This was achieved through a ceremony called the initiation of the 'Left and Right Eye of Horus' which in some respects seems to have been a short cut to enlightenment. So in other words this initiation was a shift from the then current level of human consciousness to Christ conscious beings.

The initiation went like this:

The first part involved the subject going beneath the Great Pyramid in order to encounter the 'Black Light Spiral'. This goes into the centre of the Earth. Many subjects actually died at this stage because this area manifested their thoughts. Many thought of what they feared and therefore created them, not able to face them and in some cases this proved fatal.

The next stage was to be taken to the King's chamber which was designed to catch the 'White Light Spiral' at its source which was also designed to filter out black light, almost like a cleansing after the first part of the initiation. The King's chamber is placed just off centre with the sarcophagus placed in such a way that when the subject lay in it, the white light would pass directly into their pineal gland. The pineal gland and also the pituitary gland in the brain is what makes up our third eye (psychic eye) which enables us to see beyond a five sense reality. Subjects would be placed into the sarcophagus for three and a half days where they would leave the third dimensional world, where we still reside today, and experience consciousness expansion before returning to their physical bodies. This stage caused the transformation of the self and reality.

The third and final stage was for the subjects to be taken to the Queen's chamber which was the stabilisation room. Once the subject had successfully passed through all three initiations they would emerge as Christ conscious beings with 'ascension' having been achieved, or at least practised.

Archaeologists have actually discovered a white crystalline powder inside the sarcophagus and scientists have learned that when a person is in an intense and deep meditative state they secrete a chemical from their body which in turn crystallises into a powder. The powder discovered in the sarcophagus by archaeologists was held at the British museum in London, UK. It is also a known fact that the sarcophagus is too big for the doorway of the chamber which can only mean that the sarcophagus was placed there at the time of construction and not as part of a burial ceremony after construction. This goes against the burial custom of the time which is another indication that the Pyramids were not used solely for burials.

Many strange things have happened over recent times to tourists inside certain areas of the great Pyramid. These have involved people being literally transported to other dimensions through a dimensional passageway and has been so much of a problem that many tunnels and internal chambers have now been closed off by the Egyptian government. This you are able to research for the full details.

This was the real and true purpose of the great Pyramids of Giza, an initiation and not a burial ceremony. This will raise many eyebrows and challenge many belief systems but the information that has come our way needed to be presented. It is an important revelation.

Picture of the Great pyramid and the Sphinx taken by Michael & Sarah, Egypt 2010

The Sphinx as I previously mentioned is very significant to the pyramids and is far more than what Egyptologists claim it to be, merely 'a protector'. Many claim that the Sphinx was built around about the same time as the pyramids but this has been proven incorrect and can be legitimately challenged. The Sphinx is actually one of the oldest, if not the oldest monument still standing on Earth. It is actually about

10,000 years old. We know this because the lower levels of the Sphinx have suffered water erosion damage.

Egypt was not covered by water 4000 years ago when the Pyramids were built and therefore the Sphinx must be much older than the pyramids, seeing many civilisations come and go. This monument is also very mystical and holds many ancient secrets, for instance the 'Hall of Records' which details the history of mankind and Earth and can be found in the right paw of the Sphinx.

Also it has been documented that the right shoulder of the Sphinx keeps breaking open and that the head continues to crumble. The monument is trying to reveal something to us. In the neck is a Golden spherical time capsule. There was also once an ancient civilisation of 10,000 people living beneath the monuments themselves. I don't know if they still reside beneath the surface or whether they have long gone; that to us is still unclear.

It is also believed that a large ship or what many would call a spaceship exists beneath the Sphinx. This was built as an evacuation vessel should the need have arisen to allow some to leave in a hurry, that may have been the rulers of the day or even the populous, no-one really knows, though we suspect it was probably for the rulers, actually we're convinced of it.

But before you go to Egypt with a shovel it is worth knowing that these secrets are held on a higher dimension than our own and therefore they are not on our physical realm and not currently tangible. These monuments are trying to reveal information to us, but this will only happen when human consciousness is at a sufficient level to both understand it and most importantly tolerate its higher frequency level. We simply could not cope at this point in our development with the information it holds. We can change this however depending on how quickly our consciousness develops.

If you are familiar with the story of the thirteen crystal skulls then this may resonate with you; it is also believed that beneath the Sphinx will be found the thirteenth crystal skull. There is so much we don't know about our universe and indeed our own history and ourselves. But eventually when we are capable of understanding and have raised our own consciousness sufficiently, our true power and potential will be reactivated. Then the divine abilities that lay dormant within all of us will be re-awakened and the 'True you' will emerge.

You will again be the complete all seeing, all knowing being that you really are, always have been and always will be.

CHAPTER 8:

The Oneness - How We're All Connected

Just think of that spider sitting on his web, waiting upon the invisible silk for any slight movement before the pounce. Sitting there waiting for that slight vibration, each vibration a unique message reporting back to the spider, deciphered with innate accuracy, that inner knowing. Every piece of his web connected to the other and nothing escaping attention. Interwoven and interconnected by an array of strands and patterns. A vibrational device spanning an area of space, a signal waiting for action.

This is merely a smaller version of the cosmic central consciousness, the Source, God, who we describe as 'the energy from which all else exists' and the universe is the much larger immeasurable version of the spider's web. Everything in our universe and beyond is connected like the woven silk of the spider's web and every action is noticed and heard by something or someone somewhere.

Whether we are Human, Angelic, Galactic, Cosmic, Ascended Masters, Elemental, Mammal, Fish or anything else, we are all connected to each other, everything is made of energy and all of us can tap into endless knowledge. Putting it simply, when we want to search for information these days we usually look on the internet. The internet is powered by the tower which enables us to access the font of internet knowledge. The universe is the real internet and our bodies are the tower, we are all capable of accessing all the possible knowledge out there, but we need to tune in to the correct frequencies to retrieve such material, and it isn't that difficult.

I used to ask myself how it was possible that when I silently called for a specific Angel they could hear me and duly attend my side in an instant. It took a long time for me to realise that even a mere thought is a connection, the equivalent of a personal telephone call that reaches who it was intended for. And all because all things are part of the universal 'Oneness' and therefore all things are joined energetically together. Every thought we think, every word we speak, every action that we take is noticed and it is known. Telepathy is a converse and intuition is a language, we have all had experiences when we knew what someone was about to say before any words were uttered, shared a thought with someone before realising that we have had the same thought. It is because we are all the same consciousness. Expand that principle to universal size and you have that mass connection with all else because all else is also accessing the same information as you.

We are standing upon that sensitive web called our universe and we are all one creation of connected consciousness and awareness. What we do affects others and what they do affects us. We are at a stage on our planet when we are seeing more and more unusual activity, when we are feeling energetic changes that are ending relationships, causing people to leave their jobs and making people wonder just what is going on within them. The Earth's axis is shifting and as a consequence we are seeing many more natural disasters and weather seasons the likes of which are confusing. It is just change that is too big not to notice. Planets are allegedly aligning and causing ripple effects here on Earth just like the massive ripples we cause to others with nuclear weapons and alike that inevitably affect everywhere else in the universe. We need to be aware of our actions on an individual scale as well as on a planetary scale and then and only then can we be reunited with the circuitry of the cosmos. We have over many millenniums separated ourselves from the loop by our actions and deeds and now is a time of great focus and concentration from other places to assist us in the task to reunite us. We will again become part of the One, not segregated, not of the belief that we are alone. We will again reconnect ourselves to our natural state of Oneness.

Picture by Sarah: Androgynous, galactic human light being, connected to the rest of the Universe

There are many different races of beings, of different appearance and from many different places, but nevertheless they are working together under the umbrella of divinity to help us now as planet Earth and mankind ascends to the higher realms of awareness. There is so much more out there, but many of us are still of the belief that our three dimensional occupation of space is all that exists. We can say with evidence to support our claims that what we know is just a small postage stamp of knowledge. We are all linked energetically with a multitude of dimensions and a multitude of other forms of existence, which in turn is linked to universal infinity.

We are all capable of transitioning to other beings, Elementals can become Angels, Angels can become Archangels for example. It is even possible for a human to become an Archangel too, in fact it has already happened on at least two occasions. Energy can transition and change but it cannot cease to exist.

The Archangels Metatron and Sandalphon were once human beings upon Earth but made it to the dizzy heights that they now occupy. You may have noticed that these Archangels have a different ending on their names, both end with *'ON'*. This is different to all the other Archangels whose names end in *'IEL'* or *'EL'*. Michael, Raphael, Zadkiel, Gabriel, Uriel, Jophiel, Haniel, Azrael, Chamuel, Raziel, Raguel, Ariel, Jeremiel and so on. This is to mark their transition and difference.

We and many others have been saying for a long time that because Archangels, Angels and other beings of light are not of the physical they can replicate themselves and be in several places at the same time. If for example one hundred people are calling for Archangel Michael from different parts of the world at the same time, he can oblige and attend to all of them.

To the scientific world this is but a theory, but it is a factual and true reflection of how things are to ourselves. They would say that this is not possible because it goes against the laws of physics. But now scientists have carried out experimentation with photons and their beams of light and have seen for themselves these photons naturally splitting and replicating themselves several times. This proves what we have been saying, and as for the laws of physics, well they need to be re-written. This is a science not yet discovered and many revelations that come into the genre of a spiritual nature are still awaiting and will shock the scientific world, watch this space.

When Jesus was observed to do miracles, they were not miracles, they are what we are all capable of doing, they were feats that we can all do, because we can do anything. So called miracles are a natural state of being. Instant manifestation is what we once were able to do, dimensional travel was once a frequent thing for us, we are capable of all things, we just forgot.

Someone once had the audacity to stand within the walls of a crowded room and say *"the world isn't flat, it's spherical"*. History is stacked with such temerity. Just because it doesn't fit in with the conventional view of the day it doesn't mean that it isn't accurate or true.

Laughter usually prevails when a new opinion is formed but the truth will always be the truth no matter what anyone says or believes and it takes a strong will of iron to go against the flow, to swim against a stream. This bravery is sometimes needed and justified when you hold a strong enough belief that you are right.

What is science? It is an idea analysed to the point of logical fact from which evidence is formulated and presented to the rest of us. But science is kinetic, it never stops developing new ideas that always become the new stance of the scientific world. Opinions are formed as a result of this new evidence and it results in new literature, teachings and a shelf full of new books with radical idealism.

To me, the spiritual path is a science that is yet to be discovered. In the forests of Borneo two new previously undiscovered species of animal are found each month. To conventional science they do not exist until they are seen by a physical pair of eyes or a piece of sophisticated machinery to be later examined by a scholar or professor within this genre, a great scientific mind.

This then becomes acceptable because it's conventional, there is evidence, there is nothing that can bruise an ego when a new orthodox species is seen and no-one minds sticking their necks out for a believable form of life. No-one ever minds 'playing it safe'.

Why is it that when we say that we see Angels, Ascended Masters, Cosmic Beings, Spirit Guides, Elementals, Earthbound Spirits (ghosts) and family members who exist on another level of consciousness, that we are mistaken, that we are convincing ourselves of something that cannot possibly exist? Because convention fails to recognise it, yet it proves that there are other existence's out there and that we are not alone. Isn't this just yet another form of life, a consciousness we have simply forgotten about as a result of the 'veil of amnesia' that accompanies us when we incarnate on Earth in the physical?

If we see them and we talk to them are they not real? Are my eyes not valid because I see that which is unorthodox? Is an eye witness testimony not acceptable to science just because it doesn't resonate with their logical thought process?

It seems that some of us are simply just not ready for a greater truth. Some are uncomfortable with facts that they don't necessarily understand or want to understand at this point in time.

We have all set our 'spiritual awakening' alarm clocks, but we have set them to go off at a time that is unique to us, for a time in which we want to wake up, in a different time to most others. Until that day when our alarms ring, some of us will remain on snooze.

Our beliefs, our truths and the joys that greet us every day shall remain the truth of those who realise it to be the truth until the rest of humanity is ready to acknowledge that we are not alone.

Everyone lives by their own truth, they find comfort in whatever they resonate with. This is a free will planet, but you can only have free will if you realise that you have a choice. Society today, in the main, tells us that we live in the only reality that exists. We see it as our role to make as many people as possible realise that there is a choice and that there are many realities not just ours.

The beings of light, that represent life as we don't know it are always with us and around us. We all have Guardian Angels from the point of physical birth to the point of physical death. We all have interchangeable spirit guides that help us on our life's path and soul journey and we all have tickets to all possibility because that is the true state of being we are. To Sarah and I, our reality is but one reality of infinite realities, many of which occupy the same space, living parallel with one another. We cannot go back to the misunderstanding that we are a single island hidden by an eternal sea, we are a member of a universal team and our family are amongst the stars.

When you see, sense and feel the presence of so much around you each and every day, how can we still hold onto a belief that we are the only thing to exist?

One such example of worlds beyond our own came one morning when Sarah woke up to see an Angel above us, it may have been protecting us, but whatever the reason it was clearly there. Sarah explains the event like this.

"I could hardly believe my eyes when I started to stir in the early hours of this morning. I peacefully came round and opened my eyes to see the biggest block of blue haze floating above the two of us and just below the ceiling. What happened next was even more amazing as I started to see an Angelic looking feathery wing appear through the haze. The wing was white and was positioned as though it was covering us, maybe protecting us while we slept? I was so amazed that I actually let the word "Whoaaa", come out of my mouth causing Mick to stir also. The apparition started to gently fade away and after telling Mick of my experience, we fell back to sleep.

We often call in the Angelic realm of the highest good to be with us throughout the day and night and this was a nice reassurance that they actually are there with you... even if you cannot always see them. Could it have been Archangel Michael identifying himself through his colours? Or maybe it was a member of the Blue Lightning Angels that work closely with Michael? Either way, it felt like a beautiful presence that was there to reassure and protect. It was my birthday so this was a very nice birthday present indeed"

Another such example is when one day Sarah and I were driving to a funeral and I felt really down and negative which was affecting my mood. I asked silently in my head for Archangel Michael to remove any lower energies from me. Seconds later as I looked down I saw a blue energy swirling around me at various points of my body up and down my right arm and elsewhere. I felt much better after this energetic cleansing and all I had done was to connect with Archangel Michael by telepathic thought and he appeared. It was that simple.

We are all connected to our Spirit guides too and Sarah and I listen to their ideas and intuitive messages. As previously mentioned, we all have Spirit guides, helpers from the other side, invisible to most, but beneficial to all. Some of us have family members, cosmic beings, those we don't know and even animal guides helping us each and every day in our lives, making it their business to find the answers to many of our questions and guiding us to better eventualities and more suitable outcomes.

Have you ever had thoughts in your head and think, "*where did that come from, that's a good idea I'm glad I thought of it*"? Do you ever have images in your mind's eye that you didn't put there but just seemed to fit what you were pondering? Well maybe that's your spirit guides communicating in a way they know best. Just like humans have differing methods of communication, so do your spirit guides. Sometimes with words, sometimes with feelings, sometimes with no response from us but nevertheless they continue to try.

Sarah and I have a mixture of guides, paternal and maternal grandparents, cosmic beings from Sirius and the Pleiades, a lion and lioness that we keep seeing and I even have former pets with me, all helping in different ways. Our physical bodies are vessels that enable us to experience a physical existence. What lies beneath that physical body, your soul, is eternal, after that, what awaits you may be 'beyond the physical'.

As you reach a new stage in your spiritual development and your existing guides have done all that they can for you, you may get a new shift so to speak and get new Spirit guides who are developed enough themselves to take you and guide you to the next level and next stage of your soul journey. That is where Sarah and I are now, and we have just recently been given new Spirit guides who are going to be useful to us in our new ventures, in the next phase of our journey.

Sarah has a new guide named Lou, who when in the physical resided in the USA, his human experiences will stand her in good stead for the future as she is following a similar path to what he himself did as a physical being. He told her that she is 'safe' to follow the same path as him.

I met one of my new guides for the first time just recently. His name is Mark Lehman and he was an engineer in the 1920s - 1930s and had excellent problem solving abilities, to such an extent that his work colleagues and others would always approach him to get solutions to their problems. He would always come up with an answer and he had the skill base to do just that. He informed me that I would also get many solutions and good ideas from him during the course of our unity.

He is with me now as a useful guide capable of sending me many ideas and solutions to my questions. He has already sent many answers to me in the form of channelled words. I was talking to an ex engineer recently, having a general spiritual conversation with him and some of the things I was saying didn't seem to be my words or my sentence structures. This fitted into place much more when the ex- engineer stated that I was using engineering terminology when I spoke to him. I have no knowledge of engineering and certainly am not aware of the terminology used by them within this industry. But my new guide obviously did, and knew how best to help me to reach out to the person I was speaking to with words and phrases that he could relate to and understand.

You yourself may have already been a Spirit guide or you may even be spirit guide next time around for someone else. The life experiences that you gain during this incarnation on Earth may well be beneficial to another soul in the future when they find themselves in a physical body and a physical realm of existence. You too could be helping others in the way that our spirit guides are helping us now, wanting to be heard and wanting to just help out.

Below are images of our new spirit guides, drawn for us by a spiritual channelling artist:

Sarah's spirit guide Lou

Mick's spirit guide Mark Lehman

So become aware of your helpers, say hello to them and ask them to send you the answers to your questions and solutions to your problems and they will make it their business to find out for you, if they don't happen to already know themselves. Meditate and ask for some information on your guides and see what comes into your mind, you'll be amazed as a new friendship and working relationship blossoms.

We have so much help and support around us, if we only knew this fact we would be much happier and comforted, we are not alone and you are not alone, together we have a brilliant team behind us.

We used to believe that all things needed their own box, believed that all things celestial worked separately, we were wrong. What we now know is that no matter what name these higher level inter-dimensional beings are given, usually by mankind, they too work closely together in times of divine missions. Archangels and Angels work with Galactic beings, who in turn work with Ascended Masters who in turn work with all else, it is a group effort and humankind is included in that fact.

Commander Ashtar of the Galactic Federation of Light works closely with Ascended Master Jesus or Sananda as he is known cosmically. This is such a fantastic time to be around, never before have we had so much assistance with us. Now is the time to lift ourselves towards the higher realms of consciousness. Now is the time to achieve enlightened status, that is what we really are, we just need to remember the greatness that is us. Let's return ourselves to the oneness that humankind and planet Earth are, and let's once again complete the universal circuit that we hold the fuse to.

We are all conduits that enable energy to flow through us, connecting Earth to sky, the same energy that powers all else, it is within us and a part of us, it is us. We are all the same, we are infinite consciousness connected to everyone and everything else.

CHAPTER 9:

Children Of The Stars - A Divine Mission

We are living in monumental times on the Earth at the moment. There is much coming and going and things happening on a scale that we have never before seen. The transition from this world into our new one is happening before our very eyes, piece by piece. Systems of control being dismantled before us, authorities exposed for their deliberate wrong doings, our leaders being caught out for acts of fraudulence and crimes against humanity. We are in part, seeing much of this starting to come about, but there is so much more to follow.

So is all of this happening now by coincidence or are there, as mentioned in previous chapters, other forces also at work helping to bring this about? To bring the truth of our world to our attention, to help us to comprehend just how far down the garden path we have been led and then, to show us a better way? Yes there are! As well as those already mentioned in this book, such as the Angelic realm, the Galactic realms and others, there are many beings right here in human bodies assisting at this time with Earth and her people's transformations.

These beings are on a divine mission from the stars and elected to be here at this time because they knew that given the chance, they could make a difference. As stated, you may be one of them. Your child could be one of them. Not all of these souls are conscious of this fact once incarnated onto Earth but they just follow their gut instincts, their intuition through life and this guides and directs them to exactly where they need to be or to what they need to do in order to fulfil their life's mission. There are certain characteristics with these beings that may allow them to be identified, but as there are different groups that the souls can belong to, characteristics can vary. We don't like to give name tags to things because everything just is what it is, but for the sake of making the understanding of some of these groups easier, we have categorised them to explain more about them. Although the chapter is entitled *'Children of the stars'* we mean this in the sense of us all being children, not necessarily just the little ones. In the eyes of the universe, we are all children and we are forever learning here at our Earthly school. These souls were approached by Ascended Masters, Spiritual high councils and alike to assist Earth now during the times of transformation. They were asked to help and impart their love, knowledge and wisdom to readdress the balance of negative and positive energy, as the dark souls of the planet got carried away in their roles and have gone too far. The Masters themselves have delayed their own rightful passage to permanent residence in the higher realms so that they can maintain a hands on approach with Earthly affairs. Some of them also chose to incarnate into physical bodies.

There are beings that are from other planets and galaxies of existence, some physical, some non-physical, also incarnated on the Earth today. Many would refer to these as ET's or extra-terrestrials but when they are incarnated in this way they are referred to as Starpeople or Starseeds. They are very calm and collected and have been used to a tranquil atmosphere where they are from. They came here to help because Earth is such a violent and damaging planet that they were asked to take on human bodies in order to spread their calm and kindness in turn to help diffuse the violent ways on Earth as what we do here, has a ripple effect inwards and outwards They are not used to such negative ways and often find that they cannot watch the news or read a newspaper for example because it is too upsetting for them to see what we are doing to each other on this planet. They don't really like being in the lime light and instead prefer to work from behind the scenes so to speak. They seek no recognition for the things they do as it comes natural to them and they see that if Earthlings did things in a similar manner, there would be a lot less suffering, if any in our world.

The Starpeople are often interested in UFO's and the universe and sometimes long to just go 'home', wherever home is. They may seem socially awkward and even look or act in a strange manner as they are not used to Earth life. For many, this is very new to them and uncomfortable. Sometimes they can seem as though they are being cold as they don't get emotionally involved in certain situations due to seeing a logical and reasonable solution to many problems. Therefore they have no need to be pulled into other's dramas, especially when they can see that they can easily be solved without any attachment or unneeded and unwanted attention. They are particularly against any nuclear projects on Earth as they know what damage can be done using such technology, not just on our planet. They show genuine kindness whenever possible, even in the most trivial of circumstances in the hope that this will rub off on others. This is what they have come for; this is their role in the bigger picture.

Sometimes we come across people in our lives who have a certain look about them. You can look into their penetrating eyes or listen to them speak and be completely captivated by them, drawn in by their personal gravitational pull. In children, they seem wise beyond their years and in adults, their eyes tell you a thousand stories. They have been there, done it and got the t-shirt. They have seen it all. These particular energies are said to be the 'Wise ones'. They have had many past lives on Earth as Sorcerers, Wizards, High-Priests and Priestesses and Shamans for example and have been called out of retirement so to speak, in order to assist in Earth's current dilemma. They are a font of knowledge and have a wealth of experience behind them from previous Earth lives as well as their lives in spirit where they have created beautiful realities to live in and be part of. They can seem intense and can be very eccentric with an air of mystery about them. If you try lying to a Wise One forget it! They'll know, they can see straight through it. Energy speaks louder than words to these individuals.

The Wise Ones learned to harvest their spiritual gifts in their many past lives on Earth and as such were able to channel their energy to perform amazing feats including healing and manifestations. They are highly intuitive and these magicians were able to affect the weather and move objects by telekinesis. They are extremely powerful and their help and experience is greatly needed at such an energetically dense time on Earth to help see us through. The Wise Ones were highly proficient in the psychic arts and lived lives in times such as Atlantis, ancient Egypt, and as Mayans and native medicine men and women. They know what humans are capable of and want humanity to realise this too. They have come to teach us about peacefulness and to show us how to use our inner power for the good of all.

Then there are Angels in human bodies, literally. Again, they may or may not be aware of it. These Angelic helpers in human form love so much and see the glowing potential each person possesses. They have come to infuse love onto planet Earth and again in the hope that it will rub off on its occupants. If we genuinely loved each and every living thing unconditionally, then we would solve all of Earth's problems. The Angels often end up in abusive or un-requiting relationships as they are drawn to certain people because they believe they can help that person. With these beings, beauty is much more than skin deep. They see straight past a person's physical make up and appreciate what they have on the inside. They are very sensitive and often absorb the energy of those around them, especially if involved in energy healing work. For this reason the incarnated Angelic being needs extra energetic protection to shield them as much as possible from harsh energies and should remember to clear themselves regularly of this unwanted energy.

The Angelic human can find it hard to say "*no*" to people's requests as they just want to help and feel they have to do as much as possible for people, even if it means putting themselves out. For this reason they can often be taken advantage of for their kind and helpful nature. Bottom line is though, they just want to be free to spread love and see it returned, not just to them but to everyone and everything. Something we need desperately on this Earth.

Another group of beings that elected to incarnate into physical human bodies are those of the Elemental kingdom. The Elementals include legendary beings such as the Gnomes, Elves, Fairies, Unicorns and those of the animal kingdoms. Elemental beings can look similar to their namesake and took the decision to incarnate as human's so that they could help humans to understand the pain the Earth and nature are in because of humanity's actions and disregard towards her. These fiery tempered energies are often angry towards humans for damaging the planet in such a way that also causes devastation to other worldly kingdoms that are present. They are very much at one with nature and will often prefer to be around animals than humans! They enjoy being outdoors and can be very cheeky and mischievous. The Elementals are known for having fun and certainly enjoy any practical jokes.

The Elemental humans, as well as teaching us to respect all of nature, are here to show us how to have fun. They can be very rebellious but know that joy and laughter need to be infused in our everyday living. Humanity as a race can be so serious and puts itself under immense stress and pressure. We have forgotten how to laugh and sometimes if we could just step back and take a look at ourselves and not be afraid to laugh, it would probably do us the world of good.

There are many different groups incarnated on this planet at the moment. Each has their own purpose or tasks and many perform these unconsciously. It is ingrained in their very nature and so sometimes all anyone has to do is just *be*. But sometimes more effort is needed and so sometimes when a soul suddenly finds that they have awoken or become conscious of who they truly are and why they are here, they find themselves on a very important mission. Some have been tasked with taking the bull by the horns and getting their hands dirty. This can be said of the next group of souls.

There is a generation often referred to as 'the Indigos'. The Indigos have been around for a number of years and their influence is now stronger than ever. Indigos are said to be called as such, because that is literally the colour of their aura. They are highly sensitive souls and have somewhat of a fiery spirit. They are often psychic, feel like they don't belong or don't fit in, feel different from others, have an innate feeling that they are here for a specific purpose and can't stand old structured, backwards and senseless systems. They are not keen on authority either and are truth seekers. They can see a better way of doing things and are often labelled as having Attention Deficit Hyperactivity Disorder (ADHD) as they can be so clever that they can see what they are being taught in school as being pointless and boring.

It is said that the 'mission' of the Indigo is to bring down old, non-serving and unjust systems of control and authority. Not to cause anarchy, but to make way for a new and better way. They are symbolically hacking away with a machete at anything that is no longer serving or right for humanity. This in turn is making way for another new generation of human being known as the 'Crystal children' who are also very sensitive, highly psychic and telepathic as well as extremely loving and very clever. They work mostly from the right brain which is the connection to the 'out there', to the universe and the all that is, as opposed to the left brain which is structured and rigid and keeps us very much in this three dimensional, unmalleable world. They are very creative and can be late speakers in childhood. This is because of their telepathic abilities and so they will often try and communicate mind to mind with their parents and others, using their big wise eyes to capture attention. They can also be very animated and express themselves with gestures and a look in a certain direction! Again they are very often labelled as having ADHD.

Mick recalls a time when he had a conversation with a five year old boy at a garden party one night in 2010. Mick was sitting in a chair and staring up at the stars. It was a beautiful night and very clear, ideal for letting the mind travel through space. The little boy approached and asked Mick *"What are you doing"*? with a cheeky smile on his face. Mick told him that he was just looking at the stars to which the boy replied *"Don't worry, there'll be plenty of stars when we go back home"*. The same child is also reported to have told his parents about his 'star family' whom he knew before he was born.

You see, these kids from childhood are mostly extremely clever and are a blank canvas of all possibility. It is unfortunate that many of them are misguided and instead of being encouraged with their special gifts and abilities, they are suppressed or un-nurtured. They are being deliberately targeted and distracted by the highest 'authorities' at this time and this isn't by accident. Our children, more than anyone else, are the targets of a system that fears them so immensely of being 'awake'. Why? Because our self-appointed 'authorities' are threatened by this generation's very existence. That's why they are so quick to drug children if they are 'badly' behaved. They are labelled with ADHD or some other mental illness and then administered with the kiddie cocaine known as Ritalin, in an attempt to turn them into zombies and cull their natural abilities. Children now are administered with around 26 different vaccines before the age of 6 months. This is to weaken their immune systems before it has even had chance to develop. The 'authorities' stand to lose their control over mankind as this major global awakening continues and inspires those who once lay dormant to suddenly make a difference in their own way.

It is happening and no matter what label we choose to give to these beings, they are playing a major role in the whole thing. They are inspiring those who have long forgotten who they really are and why they are on the Earth, back into action. It is a very exciting time to be alive and believe us, together we are bringing it about.

So if you feel that maybe you or your children are part of this influx of positive energy, remember to nurture and not supress. Find what makes your heart sing and encourage these gifts to come out in a positive and helpful way! When way has been made for these new, fair and humane systems these generations will be the ones that show us how to live in it. How to be at peace with one another, how to love one another, how to respect one another, how treat everyone and everything as equal, how to exist in harmony just like we did many millennia ago before the great fall in consciousness.

Once again, it doesn't matter what we choose to call them. In truth, many of us may well fit the description of many of these generations but what we need now is for even more of us to wake up to this fact and start living out our purpose. We are so powerful and this power will be used for the good of all. Names are irrelevant as everyone has a part to play now, whether from one of the groups mentioned or not. Humans are special beings in themselves and they are the ones who will take planet Earth forward into her next incarnation. That is why so much is happening now, breaking down the old and making way for the new; not just the new Earth, but the new human also. We are evolving as a race and expanding into our intergalactic connections, allowing us to be in the world but also to travel outside of it, without the use of weighty technology. Everything that we could ever need is right here within us, just waiting to be activated, and all of the qualities that are mentioned of the different groups here to help, are also present within you, us and everyone else. Activation is the key!

We are all divine sparks of light in reality, no matter who we are, where we are from or what we are doing here.

This is our time to shine.

CHAPTER 10:

The Whirlwind Of Truth

Do you ever wonder what is wrong on planet Earth? Why we seem to be constantly at war with each other, people starving, people losing their homes, banks and governments filling their pockets and getting more and more personal wealth whilst all around them the people seem to be getting less and less?

Is it a coincidence that we are living in such times or has it been engineered that way? Unfortunately, there is a lot of evidence supporting the latter. But who would be so sinister as to create such disharmony and suffering for so many and why?

To know the answers to this we can look as far back as Atlantis and the times of the Golden age and even beyond. Society has always been structured so that a few people are worshipped by the populous and so that those 'blessed' few can control the many, and they do this by tricking us into policing ourselves. For example encouraging people to spy on each other and report our neighbours to the local authorities if we see them putting the wrong type of rubbish into the wrong coloured bin on the wrong day. Concentrating on the differences between us and playing us off against each other simply because we have a different belief system, and look at the world, it's working quite well for them! These few tend to be in positions of power such as royalty, governments, military, media and perhaps most importantly of all, banking, as well as those hidden in the shadows. They rely on nations to stay unaware as they work by stealth to keep people from becoming conscious. Declaring war between nations and then stepping back whilst the people fight those wars; funny how those who declare them don't go anywhere near the front line, or any line at all come to think of it. War is big money for those who declare it, but how senseless? If our armies refused to fight there would be no war. Isn't it ironic that we currently have former British Prime Minister Tony Blair, the man who took Britain into two wars, as the Middle East peace envoy. It's like having a paedophile as a child minder.

If we are conscious then there is no place for their greed and injustice or war because a conscious society is a spiritually connected society, working only from the heart and with love in everything we do. We reconnect with our true essence and reclaim our phenomenal god given abilities. Telepathy, manifestation, teleportation, love to mention but a few. No-one goes hungry, no-one goes homeless, no-one suffers all the while struggling to provide money that doesn't exist to governments and banks who seek to enslave. And no one will have to pay interest on the money that doesn't exist either. It is immoral and wholly wrong, it is legalized robbery, legal because the system makes it legal.

We can change this overnight and '*they*' know that. That is why we find things seemingly getting worse. 'They' are throwing everything at us to keep us down because 'they' know we are waking up. Put yourself in 'their' shoes. Would you want us to wake up?!

But with each day that passes, more and more people are realising that we are all one, all connected, all possibility, all love. In our new world no-one need suffer, no-one need hunger. 'They' cannot handle this, knowing that 'their' time is shortly coming to an end and their grip on power is loosening rapidly.

But who are '*they*'? Well if you were to say that they don't sound human... you'd be right, these are low vibrational inter-dimensional entities that many would call extra-terrestrial, more specifically, from the constellation of Draco and of reptilian appearance. There is much mounting evidence to support this claim. This is where the old time sayings such as 'Draconian' come from and even characters such as

Dracula, (Draco-ula). But they do use humans to further this agenda and to see the evidence of this, you need look no further than our governments; every puppeteer needs a puppet at the end of his string.

So then, what tactics do these shadow people use to darken our light and keep us oblivious? Well in truth there are so many. But one such tactic we'd like to draw your attention to is Codex Ailmentarious (Global food code). Have you ever heard of Codex Ailmentarious? No, neither had Sarah and I, and that's what those behind it are banking on.

"*You can fool some of the people all the time, and those are the ones you want to concentrate on*" - President George W Bush - *March 2001*.

There is an ill wind heading towards humankind in relation to our food and our water, a life essential that can be manipulated into a sure guarantee of wide scale contamination. Sarah and I have discovered that sometime in 2011 there is to be an EU (European Union) directive to ban alternative healing with herbs and all things good for us and in addition to that to ban all books relating to this subject. There are also plans to make all vitamins prescription only. No more will we be able to go to our local pharmacy and buy them over the counter. This has already come into force in many areas of the United States of America where the farming of self-grown natural food has been banned and people have even been prosecuted for growing their own cucumbers!

Things that are naturally good for our welfare and wellbeing are being taken away from us. Why? If medication worked why are so many people unwell? We are made to be unwell by all the opposition we face. On this Earth there is a natural cure for every illness, but if we were allowed to find it and use it then pharmaceutical companies would be out of business. For instance it is said by a few well-placed doctors that cancer, which is an acidic fungi, can be cured by something as natural and simple as bicarbonate of soda, which is an alkaline and reverses the effects of this disease. It has worked on many cancer sufferers, but we never hear about it. And there is much talk of Flaxseed oil doing the same thing, another natural remedy. But we advise everyone to do their own research into these remedies as it is more complex than to simply take them as a medicine. There are special techniques involved and those administering them are experts in this field.

There seems to be an attack on public health on a large scale by the authorities, a self-awarded description and title. Big pharma, those that make billions each year from medications, have spoken and the politicians must comply if they want to maintain their positions of power. Even the governments themselves have admitted in writing the fact that right now, not all products are labelled as genetically modified even if they are. How can we choose what to eat if we aren't told what we are eating? Genetically modified food is designed to genetically modify us, from the inside out.

Laws are stealthily being introduced to make injections, especially in relation to the vaccination of children, compulsory. Injections that contain harmful substances that have in some cases in the UK at least resulted in death, but of course... there is never any connection! Doctors are being paid bonuses each time they administer the swine flu injection, to give them incentive to do so. And now even the yearly Flu vaccine contains the swine flu ingredients. The swine flu vaccine contains mercury, a known poison to the human body.

The system has a hold on us. Each child that is born in the UK now instantly has a £200,000 debt as a result of the global banking situation, so even our children are weighed down as soon as they are born. As we become more enlightened the system gets more desperate and they attempt to introduce their agenda much quicker. They are trying to build as many snowmen as they can before the snow melts and things are speeding up and are being rushed through. This is encouraging because that means that all is not going to plan for them.

In a so called democratic world why doesn't anyone ever ask us? Don't we have a choice, and don't *you*? The people only get in the way of this pre-ordained agenda. We can protest and argue but we never get the choice, because it is already in place before we often even know about it.

Look into all that we have said, because it affects every single one of us, especially those who practice and teach alternative methods. We are going to change this situation, we are going to overthrow this madness, but fasten your seatbelts for the bumpy ride! We are very spiritual individuals and we are passionate about the Mind, Body and Spirit aspect of our lives. But beware, because to the agenda it means this: Controlling your MIND, Damaging your BODY and Weakening your SPIRIT! They will not succeed.

Don't be told what to do, break free, you are all powerful and magnificent beings of light, let's all shine together. Humans beings are all possibility, we are all that is, was and ever will be. We are all part of an endless universe, which in turn connects to other endless universes. We are all on a journey of consciousness expansion and soul growth, trying to reach the highest of realms by many life times of experiences, as many different individuals within a different shell that is our human body for that period. On this occasion our experience is Michael and Sarah Feeley, but the real us goes far beyond the names we are given for this incarnation on Earth. We reside upon a beautiful planet that contains a magnificent soul that like each and every one of us is awakening at a rapid pace. We are all conduits connecting father to mother, that is heaven and Earth and every one of us has a special unique part to play. We chose to play our part, and as it says in the Movie the *Matrix "You've already made the choice. Now you have to understand it"*. In other words by actually being here now, you have chosen to be here. Now you have to awaken and answer the question of why? We all have a role to play. And then you will be able to answer the question that we have all asked ourselves, who am I and why am I here?

Archangel Azrael once said to me *"If you could remember where you came from, we would have difficulty convincing you to stay down here"*. As all possibility, we can do, think and be anything we want, we can manifest our path and our future by positive thoughts and vision because we live in the now which is all that is. When you think of the past you are in the now, when you think of the future, you are in the now. The space that is 'now' contains all of those possibilities.

But society wants anything but all possibility and it therefore gives us many different un-important things to focus upon, and as a result of doing just that you then become just one possibility. You are in effect, limiting yourself and focusing on one thing working within a small box that you have created for yourself.

Celebrity icons, musical hero's, TV personalities, last week they were unknown and easily passed in the street but this week they are famous and are now a figure of worship. We look up to and admire those who are only equal to us, yet this puts us on the tide that takes us in the opposite direction from where we need to be. It takes our focus elsewhere, we are now limited. Enjoy these things but see them for what they really are, a bit of fun.

It's a sense of priority. We have things the wrong way round. We look small when we should be looking big because we are big. The postage stamp that is your new pedestal is now a limiter for your consciousness and you only work within its remit, you have lost a sense of all possibility that is you and everyone. And the system creates perfect surroundings to keep you in this belief. Break free of limiting beliefs, break free of any small boxes, you are part of an endless space, a space large enough to allow any consciousness to expand beyond your wildest dreams, beyond the scope of conventional understanding. Let us acknowledge our potential, let us marvel in the greatness that is us. As we have said many times, we are brilliant beings of light, let us shine, let us realise that all possibility is a massive space in which to operate within. Everything is thrown at you to prevent this from happening, even laws are passed to control you and your every movement.

Common law was enshrined in the Magna Carta in 1215 when King John was forced to sign it. It became the law of the land, and still remains to this day in the UK. Many criminal offences are encompassed within this law, even Murder. Common law is basic, as long as you don't breach the peace, hurt anyone, cause any damage to another's property or belongings or cause its loss, you will not have breached this law. A simple system that traces back to Celtic times when we lived in tribes. We can in effect still create our own laws under the law of the land namely 'Common law'. This was never written out of the British constitution the 'Magna Carta'. The use of Common law is the use of common sense and does not need statutory laws to tell us what to do, or even force us, as is now the case.

Common law changes gradually over time and therefore this slow process is of no use to the secret societies who currently control our planet. They are relatively few in number. Therefore they needed a system of law to speed up the process in order to create a faster control system. That was of course 'Statutory Law'. So now we have statutory law. Rules and legislation can be drawn up quickly even without any debate or public consultation, how many times do we see this today? Before you know it, it has become law, it is now in force and we the people were not even told about it. Common law refers to the actual human living being whereas Statute law refers to the corporations, big industry and ultimately a power base. We have now become a corporate entity and we are no longer seen as the human being, because those who created this system needed to wrought fake corporations or 'persons' in which to apply their newly created laws and that includes you.

Just look at all your own official documents, your name is normally written in capitals, they are not writing to you, the living being, they are addressing the fake 'strawman' that was created when you were born. They keep you believing throughout your life that the two are the same thing when they are definitely not.

The 'Royal' crest depicting a Lion wearing a crown and a Unicorn. The Lion represents 'royalty' and the powers that be. The Unicorn represents enlightenment and the people. Note how the Unicorn has a chain around its neck and body – a symbol of subservience and of being stifled.

From Statute law we also have Maritime law (law of the sea and also known as Admiralty law as well as other names), which covers the sea and now crosses over onto the land because they needed to amalgamate both to gain control of all. To meet the criteria of Maritime law every person in effect represents a ship. When you see the Gold border around a flag, you know that is it operating within Maritime law. There are many words that we use today that obviously refer to Maritime law, for instance at court you stand in the 'Dock'. We also have for example: *PartnerShips, RelationShips, LordShips, LeaderShips, ScholarShips, FriendShips, FellowShips,* to name but a few.

And then of course you have your 'berth' (birth) certificate, just as a ship must be in possession of when it docks.

This is a direct quote from Jordon Maxwell, who is a leading American researcher on this subject, which fits in nicely with what we are saying, albeit he is referring to America, it is still in effect correct for the rest of the world:

"When you are born you come out of your Mothers water, therefore you must have a Birth certificate, a certificate of manifest, because you are a corporation owned item. You are a human resource. This goes back to the German Nazi concept that every human coming out of their mother's water must be 'berthed' (See Maritime law). Therefore, you have to have a certificate of manifest to see how much this individual is going to make for us in our new world order.

I am telling you that until you understand the laws, the symbols, emblems and what these words mean, you are never going to suspect how far gone we really are. Did you know, for instance, that your birth certificate is a security on the stock exchange on the New York stock market? Did you know that? ... on all birth certificates in this country... on the right hand corner, you will always have a series of red numbers... those are a security number on the world stock exchange.

Go to any good stock office and ask them to check these numbers in the computer and see what this stock is worth. They will check it on the New York stock exchange and find you. Your birth certificate is a stock on the stock exchange in America. Why? Because you are worth money to the international banks... we need to wake up. This is serious stuff".

So how does this fit into our spiritual aspect and view on things. Well if you were not enslaved by these fake and unjust laws, if you were allowed to shine and become the 'All possibility' that is you then you would be the complete enlightened being you are capable of becoming. It is these systems that are blocking our growth. If we were not the subject of such blockages, then limitations holding us down would no longer be. The awakening is changing all of this and the more people that know about it the more people will become enlightened to the 'All that is'. We are infinite beings of consciousness. We are freedom and that is why the system strives to keep us down... because it does not want us to realise it. It is throwing everything at us but it is all in vain.

Things are changing, the secrets we have been so oblivious to are becoming apparent, let's keep up the good work! It is all starting to come out, we are becoming aware of these chains around our necks. Together we are so bright that we can be seen across the spectrum of our galaxy, we can show ourselves to be worthy of cosmic help and we can reconnect this wonderful planet Earth to the 'Oneness' she and all of us are a part of. Switch on your light and be seen and others will follow you.

There is an energetic change on its way to planet Earth, some call it the truth vibration, some call it the love vibration, nevertheless it is what it is. When this energy reaches us and it is already starting to, you and everyone else will notice the affects. This energy will bring to the surface things that were once hidden, things that were kept secret from us, and it is already occurring. How many times do we now see the wrongdoings of our politicians and people of power being exposed? Once they could hide the truth from us but now it is becoming more and more difficult and this is just the beginning. Let's all prepare and enjoy the whirlwind of truth as it stirs the seabed in order to cleanse all the hypocrisy and deceit that we have all been the victim of.

When the spiritual path grabs you, when you begin to see and recognise the game plan, and the forces of good and bad that exist, your eyes develop x-ray vision; x-ray vision by virtue of the fact that you can see straight through it. It's like a game of chess, once you learn the moves of both black and white, you are better positioned to play the game. When you know what moves are likely to be made next you can counteract them. Do you not want to be *free*, immune to being ruled?

You see, we live in times of control, control, control. There is an agenda going on, but our focus is being distracted by materialistic possessions, by a selfish morality. The air I breathe, the food I eat, the water I drink is changed by the unnatural ingredients added to it.

Our world is controlled by secret societies who recruit talented 'yes men and women' who are more than willing to forward the agenda. The masonic signs are everywhere, the black and white chequered band on the British police uniform is such a symbol, and that is just one example. Presidents who read pre-written lines from autocue, not from the heart, it is the words of another deluding us into a false belief, from those who control us from behind the scenes... and some of them are not even human! But thankfully they are relatively few in number and that's why they have to control from behind the scenes.

Their agenda includes de-population; there are just too many humans on Earth for them to control and they see themselves as the rightful rulers of our planet. Just look at the Georgia Guide Stones, which tell us that the plan is to maintain Earth's population at below 500,000,000 people. Even his royal virus... ahem, excuse me, highness, Prince Phillip of the British 'royal' family said in 1988 upon being asked what he would like to came back as if he reincarnated: *"In the event that I am reincarnated, I would like to return as a deadly virus, to contribute something to solving overpopulation"*. So blatant!

When you know this, when you know how their mind set works, you can see the chess pieces being moved. You can see that so called accidents that result in the death of thousands are not really accidents, they are sometimes the workings of the agenda. Other plans on the list of many include globalisation, a new world order (NWO). Even former British prime-minister Gordon Brown used this terminology and phrase many times and it was well documented. He even stated in public that he wanted to help put the new world order into place and that he saw it as his post government task and role.

In the coming months and years, and you can already see it happening, the plan is to have central control of everything and everyone, a world bank, maybe the International Monetary Fund (IMF) renamed of course, but nevertheless still the IMF. Why so many bank bail outs? It is a manufactured bubble of debt, burst deliberately and even the stock markets are manufactured to do a certain thing at a certain time. If you ever want to know when something big is about to happen just look at the activity on the stock markets and you will see a pattern emerging, as if someone somewhere knew something was about to happen beforehand, and they did, because it was planned that way. For instance the recent BP oil disaster is a perfect example.

You can see this with all the bail outs of sovereign countries, Greece, Ireland and soon possibly Spain, Portugal and then many others until we are all forced to become one, a global bank, a global army, a global government and it is developing very quickly. Then the few can control the many. The agenda has sped up because more and more people are waking up and with this, the power of the agenda, and those behind it, who rely on everyone remaining oblivious, is being chipped away.

Sarah's rendition of light overcoming and penetrating into the dark

They will try anything and stop at nothing to prevent your enlightenment, but we are not so much the target, this is of course our children, the new generation. We are the advanced party, the Indigo children, carving the way for the Crystal children who will take our planet to the next level. They for obvious reasons are the main target with vaccinations, microchips and alike causing the deliberate disruption of their immune systems before it has had chance to develop properly.

A controlled media, controlled public, so called independent inquiries, overseen and controlled by the department being investigated, need I go on? And now of course the Wikileaks scenario, maybe this is the 'False messiah' a controlled distraction aimed at causing dis-unity amongst nations or even to justify greater internet control, for 'national security' of course. Who knows, only time will tell, but we won't be too surprised if this turns out to be the case.

This agenda is however doomed! A mass awakening is occurring on a planetary scale and our enlightenment in the next few years will be so fast that any agenda of darkness will not know what has hit it. Be ready everyone, be ready and prepared for what is going to happen and prepare yourselves for this day. Make sure that all those you know are ready too.

Not long now until the whirlwind of truth reveals many things that until now have been kept secret and from us all, we the people.

The time is now.

CHAPTER 11:

A Time Of Awakening

There is evidence mounting, that the moon is a great big anomaly; an unnatural structure that has many independent and free thinking scientists baffled. Their dilemma? The moon shouldn't be there. We are told by mainstream science, that the moon is probably a great big chunk of the Earth that broke off many millennia ago after being struck by a meteorite of some kind. They called this theory, the whack theory. They then concluded that this wasn't correct and that the meteor, to have caused such devastation must have come back for another go and struck the Earth again which then resulted in the satellite known as our moon. This, they called, the double whack theory!

More and more research is being conducted into the moon mystery and more and more anomalies keep appearing. You only need to put 'who built the moon' or 'spaceship moon' or words to that effect into an internet search engine to reveal the wealth of information on this subject. Alternative evidence tells us that the moon is actually a giant spacecraft of sorts and was flown across the universe by two brothers who were part of the Annunaki, a technologically advanced, malevolent group of extra-terrestrials who came to Earth a long time ago to mine for gold. In the process, they genetically manipulated the human race and in effect made humans a slave race, using them to do the work for them. They exerted control over the populous at first overtly, but when the people rebelled, the Annunaki retreated and started to operate from behind the scenes and began using genetically modified human puppets to do their dirty work for them and to keep the populous in line. These puppets eventually took up positions of power such as those in royalty, banking and politics etc, and still reside there today, from where they pull their invisible strings.

It is said that when the moon was flown into the Earth's atmosphere, this is what caused the great flood talked about in the bible and other ancient texts. The arc was possibly more of a submarine type structure carrying the genetic codes for each and every life form. There is a reason that the moon was positioned in the way it was. In contrast, our sun plays an important role for us spiritually. It sends out informational photon energy which activates the pituitary and pineal glands in our brain. This, in effect is what makes up the third eye chakra, our psychic eye that enables us all to see beyond a five sense reality and into other dimensional worlds. Much awaits us beyond this curtain that we currently cannot see, but nevertheless, it is there. To see all would be our natural state of being. Without this we can only see beyond the five senses if we boost our signals by awakening spiritually using the enlightenment that we all are, and of course, everything is stacked against us to prevent this too.

The sun, when active emits sunspots, sun explosions and activity, causing heat waves amongst other things and includes the delivery of informational photons. So if there was a force that wanted to keep humanity asleep and un-awakened, then a good course of action would be to somehow block or divert these photonic signals, and by doing so would keep the majority of humanity within the illusory five sense reality that we mostly currently reside in. So how could these spiritual and photon signals be blocked? For the answer to this we need look no further than... you guessed it! *The moon.*

From the moon, interference is beamed out into space that block out the signals from the sun's photon energy and consequently jam our third eye (psychic eye) and stops us from seeing beyond our three dimensional 'reality'. This keeps many believing that this is the only reality, when, *in reality*, this is only just the start. NASA knows, although they won't tell you, that on the dark side of the moon there are extra-terrestrial bases. We can see evidence of this on leaked photographs of the moon from insiders, in which the images show large structures which can clearly be observed. These are obviously not man made as *we* know it. The moon has a significant effect on Earth, it makes the tides go in and out, it affects our bodies and the cycles we go through and when there is a full moon, it clearly affects people mentally. We know from our experience as police officers that when there is a full moon, many people seem to act crazy! In this way they are said to be acting like lunatics or 'lunar-tics'. The moon, as beautiful as it may appear in all of its glory in the night sky, clearly has an effect on us that we would be much better off without.

Clearly, there is much to be uncovered about the moon and its relationship with Earth's current state of affairs but this is part of what will eventually be revealed. Remember, even some scientists accept now, that the moon isn't what we think it is.

There has been much speculation about the famous year 2012, in films, news, documentaries and not least the Mayan calendar. 2012 is a year just like 2013, 2014 and so on. Whatever is purported to happen then, is already happening now. It is a gradual process of awakening; the veil is getting thinner and thinner between our world and many other worlds. More people today are seeing things that they cannot explain of a paranormal and supernatural nature and they are feeling things that they have never before felt. People's senses are awakening and this is just going to continue on through 2012 and beyond as humanity goes through its process of transformation.

At this time, it will help to be as spiritually aware as possible, regardless of what does or does not happen. One possibility, in our view, having researched certain pieces of information both spiritual and scientific, is that in the coming years the sun, which is currently in an inactive state not seen for a long time, is going to become active once again. Very active. This activity will emit large and powerful sun spots that will override any deliberate blockages caused by the position of, and interference from the moon. When this happens our third eye will be exposed to the effects of the informational photon energy that will in turn allow us to see, and maybe in many cases, instantly, all that is around us, on this dimension and others, good and bad and all that hides beyond the available light of our physical eyes and reality.

Can you imagine this happening instantly when you are not aware of anything beyond this realm? Even for those prepared it would be a shock, so for those who are unprepared it would be an ambiguous and trying time. There is much beauty to behold, but there is also much we do not want to see and have yet to comprehend and come to terms with. This is all part of the awakening, whether it happens in this way or not. We are waking up having been pinned down for far too long. There isn't enough dark to hold the light down, that is why we are seeing things happen at a rapid rate of knots at the moment as the control system throws everything it's got at us in a last desperate attempt to keep us pinned. At the same time we are seeing these attempts fail as the new and much stronger, beautiful energies penetrate our atmosphere and strike right at the heart of the people. This is causing people to gasp with relief as they suddenly feel themselves being freed, freed from the bondage they have been unknowingly born into. This is also why the world seems to be in chaos, because it is! We have these very different agendas playing out now on the world stage and it's only going to go one way... *our way*; for the good of all, including those that have subjected us to such negativity. We are after all, going back to the same place eventually.

Many things have been set to help trigger this burst in consciousness, not least through recurring numerological sequences. Many numbers are very important to us all and have a much more significant and deeper meaning than we realise, for example the number 11. The number 11 is considered a master number in numerological terms and is a pre-encoded trigger for our DNA. It activates our cellular DNA strands which in turn accelerate our consciousness. We have a large proportion of dormant DNA that is known scientifically as Junk DNA, but if it's there, then it is there for a reason. Creation did not give us things that we didn't need or would never ever use.

A growing number of people across the world now see this number, and others, in its various sequences, such as 11, 111, 11:11. Maybe you've seen it. Maybe you are one of those that happen to see 11:11 on your digital clock too often to be a coincidence, or 1111 drive by on a cab for example. Number 7 is a popular one for us but it has more recently become the 11:11 sequence. Interestingly, but not by intention, upon writing this chapter it just so happened that it ended up as being chapter 11, a complete synchronicity.

We have also just entered the year 20-11, a significant year. This is a fantastic time to be alive and in a human body, on planet Earth at this point in her history. We all decided that we wanted to be here now. Soon our roles in the big picture will be known. Our own individual piece of a very large jigsaw will fit nicely into all the other pieces that we are yet to see. 11.11.2011 will see a new influx of divine energy, again helping and gently ensuring that our awakening continues. 11 also signifies the nearing of the end of a cycle. That is true. We are now, as a planet and as a race, closer than ever before to achieving levels of awareness not experienced for some time in our history.

In the coming years the human race will have the opportunity to transcend from its current state of duality, where everything is either black or white, good or evil, right or wrong, to its rightful state of 'Oneness', because that is how it all works. We are all one. We are all connected to everything and everyone else. Our thoughts and our actions are themselves a creation, a vibration that can be heard and sensed across our universe and beyond. Positive thoughts can be manifest into our reality, there is so much that we have forgotten. We are all that is, was and ever will be.

We are able to attract in and manifest anything we want into our lives using the law of attraction. The law of attraction is much used on other realms for creation of literally anything. We once possessed the power of manifestation where we were able to create out of thin air, using the power of thought vibration and focus, to affect the very molecules of that space. This manipulation of the molecules coupled with the 'like attracts like' positive mental attitude, allows us to pull things from the universe that our soul needs or wants to experience. As the density of the Earth dropped so did our ability to create in this way as everything became heavy and slow, but this will, and is returning.

If the collective consciousness of the human race, puts out to the universe that it wants to change the world, then we will change the world. The law of attraction not only works on an individual basis but on a collective basis. This is why it is so important that we work together collectively to bring in and be the change that we want to see. As we become increasingly aware of who we are and what we are doing here it is important to visualise what it is that we want to see. For us, we want to see a world full of beauty and vibrance, where all of humanity love's each other and their surroundings. Where there is no trace of suffering in any way and where all of our divine abilities are intact, used for the good of all; where we don't need a car to travel, or a plane to get to the other side of the world because we can just think it and be there. This is a very real possibility but we must first prove that we are responsible with it. Think positive thoughts. Let your imagination run wild! That chance is just around the corner.

We will see and feel many significant changes to our bodies and our reality because it is all changing. The way in which we see our life will appear differently to us, because now is when we will see the truth of our current reality and see it for what it is; a three dimensional theatre of dreams. Many will feel a change from within but won't necessarily know what is happening or how to interpret the changes. If this happens, has happened or is happening to you or someone you know, don't worry, it is just a natural occurrence, a natural process of preparation before you move onto something more. Our cellular structures are getting ready for something new to arrive. We are becoming the completed human package, complete with new energies to exist in our new reality.

Our many lives on Earth and other places, in which we educated our soul, was for this reason; the transition from what we are now, to what we will be again. All the hardship, struggle, good times and bad were all for a reason, to learn and to grow. And when we have mastered all that we needed to master on this realm we will move on to the next level of being. Everything is just a different level of awareness and consciousness and we are aiming to get ourselves onto the next rung of that spiritual ladder. And we do that by experiencing all that there is to experience on each of the many levels of each incarnation.

This is a lot to take in, especially if you are new to this information. The fact remains, that if you have found this information, or information from somewhere else of the same subject, then the awakening is doing its thing. It is reaching more and more people, touching and starting them into action. It won't stop here. Once you break free of the chains, the world (and beyond) is literally your oyster, an ocean of discovery that never ends and is full of indescribable beauty. The beings that are assisting us from other places, other realms of existence tell of how they can literally see our light getting brighter and brighter. The pockets of light that they can see will continue to grow until eventually the whole world is united in consciousness.

There are many possibilities for the coming times but one thing is for certain... there is a spiritual revolution upon us. Slowly but surely, (and in some cases quite quickly), many are waking up and realising that they have been nothing more than slaves. Slaves to a system, slaves to society, slaves to a job... slaves to a faceless 'power' that dictates our every move even into the finest details of our lives. Country by country, uprising after uprising, realisation after realisation, that we, humanity, are *so much more than this*. We need to stand together, side by side, race by race and say *"NO MORE"*. No more to these slavish ways, to this slavish system. We are beautiful, infinite, precious sparks of divine life and we have come to change this planet back into the paradise that it deserves to be. We can do this together. We don't need violence we just need each other. That's it. Including those in uniforms that carry out the will of the 'authorities'. We are all in this together.

This image by Sarah, represents and depicts humanity awakening from its slumber, breaking free of the chains and returning to full consciousness

Be prepared, awaken yourselves up to all possibility and help those around you, then we can be ready, willing and able to cope with all that we are exposed to and can cater for anything that we weren't expecting.

"The grand awakening is coming. There will be many false messiahs, don't fall for their charms. Remain steadfast in your goals for a sweet outcome" - Channelled message from Commander Ashtar - *Galactic Federation of Light.*

The truth is coming out, the awakening has begun. In our life time we will all see it and our world will have changed for the better, just as we hoped when we all volunteered to bring about that change. Earth and mankind have spoken and the universe has heard us, it has listened. Enlightenment is within our grasp once again. Reach out and take hold of it, it is yours. We are almost there; our work here is nearly done.

Not long now...

CHAPTER 12:

We Are The Light, We Are The Love

We *are* the change that we want to see... We just need to *be* it. Inside every person, is a great soul, a brave being of light that decided to accompany those on the front line during their mission on Earth. When we talk of people being made of light, it is to be taken literally. When we were all created, we started out as a spark of light, separated from the cosmic central consciousness so as that we could experience. Again, some refer to this as the 'source' or 'God'. This is what it means when you hear about us all being connected and all being part of the same energy.

Every single living being, literally came from the same place. Where we were once a big mass of divine energy floating around peacefully in the ether, we are now individual, unique aspects of that same energy, experiencing 'life' in a variety of different ways. The soul longs to experience as much as possible; physically, emotionally and spiritually. We find ourselves in so many scenarios during our Earthly lives, some good and some not so good, but it may be that some of these experiences are some of the things that our soul felt it needed to experience so as to learn, grow and expand.

We are all on a journey. Some talk about the journey 'home'. This can have different connotations; are we on a journey back to the place our soul has been most comfortable at such as on another planet or dimension that we have spent much time at before our Earthly existence? Or are we talking about going back home to source, back to the all that is, the cosmic central consciousness that we all once came from? Or is it both?! It is possibly the latter as we are infinite beings of awareness and have an eternity to get where we are going... so why not enjoy the ride along the way. Once we incarnate on Earth, we enter into a cycle; a karmic cycle where all of our thoughts and actions come with a consequence, both positive and negative. The idea of life is to learn and experience, and the physical Earthly life has the added difficulty of all the emotions that we are prone to.

We must learn to master these emotions in any given situation so that we eventually go beyond the cycle, balancing out any karmic energy that we have accrued along the way. Karma is not a punishment or reward, it is simply an act of balancing out energies, cause and effect that is ours to own. For instance, if you commit a negative act that hurts someone, then the energy needs to be readdressed and you may have an experience that will help you to understand how you made that person feel. Likewise, if you do a good deed or a good turn for someone or something else, you may experience an event that helps you to understand how you helped, and makes you feel good. Karma can also be brought with you from past incarnations. Karma can appear as a punishment or reward but it isn't, it is simply the energy balancing itself out. So hopefully by the time you have finished your experience here on Earth, you won't have any negative karma to be repaid, only positive. Life is jam packed with things for us to do, no matter how we feel or what we have experienced. We can either react to a situation without thinking and hope for the best, or we can take a moment's pause and assess what moves we are going to make that will result in being for the highest good of all. And on top of all this… we must do it all with *love*. Love. Because in truth, that's all that really exists.

Love means 'level of vibrational energy' and in its highest state, it is a beautiful, pure, high vibrational resonance. The source, from which all else exists or the cosmic central consciousness, is made of one hundred percent, pure love in its highest state. And everything exists from and because of the source, so therefore, no matter who you are or what you do, you exist totally of love. To what degree of love you choose to express, is up to you but we are all capable of loving one another and everything else, with complete and utter love of the highest light and resonance. Okay, we are a little out of practice (okay we are a *lot* out of practice)! But with time, consideration and effort, we will get back to being in such a state of love that it will feel completely normal. When that time comes, and it is coming, we will take this world into new realities of existence. We all exuberate light within our very being; some have chosen to hide it and commit unruly acts, and others let it shine forth. Hence, we are the light, we are the love. So we, the souls on a mission to help Earth, with assistance from those from other places, are the way showers and we are the frontline that, with perseverance, will make, and are making a difference.

People often say that if God really cared, then why doesn't he help? Why does he leave us to suffer? The source or 'God' cannot just step in and change the world for several reasons; although we are individual pieces of this energy, in our current states we are vibrationally incompatible. If 'God' were to suddenly appear it would probably be the death of us as vibrationally it could be like a fire meets water situation. The two are so very different that unless a middle ground is met, they cannot be comfortable in each other's presence. This is why we are being sent help in the form of Ascended Masters, Angels, Galactic beings, Starseeds and so on. They are aware of the problems on Earth and the mission to reclaim her and they are of a more suitable resonance that allows them to be present to assist and make a difference. In this way the source is able to assist indirectly.

Another reason why the source will not intervene directly is because, quite frankly, this is our mess and we have either created or allowed for it to be created. We have allowed our power to be taken from us and have failed in the past to stand up for ourselves, preventing the current state of madness to occur. This is however, changing as we speak. Remember that we ultimately learn from our experiences, positive and negative and although the situation on Earth isn't a nice one, we will be taking away a lot from this harsh classroom of learning. Hopefully then, we will use this knowledge to continue to change the world for the better and use it as a measure of what we want, and what we don't want, in our new emerging world. We will be using this experience in times to come when we return to other levels of the ether or even other planets and using it to assist others in a similar predicament to our own. And what's more, we will be telling these souls of how we changed our world, how we made a difference by standing up and being counted and refusing to bow down to tyranny. We are divine teachers in the making.

So this is the journey. We cannot go directly back to source. We must first purge ourselves and we have an eternity to do it. Life is what you make of it so strive for the very best and if you don't get it, just know that what you are learning in the process is food for the soul.

We have been asked many times *"what is ascension"*? *"What is enlightenment"*? To us, both are simply realising that there is so much more to existence and life than we currently acknowledge. When you realise this, you start to take yourself out of the cycle that is keeping you down and that naturally leads to the beginnings of enlightenment; the seeds have now been planted. You begin to look from the outside in. You have started that journey of activating your greatness and the abilities that you have lying dormant. You are becoming enlightened and you are becoming the real you once again. And adding to that, at the point that your vibrations begin to increase to higher levels of awareness, you are beginning to 'ascend'. It is that simple, it is that easy and all that you need now and forever more is held within you and you have the power and authority to activate it. Each and every one of us *is* that magnificent. Do your best to better yourself and your own path and make sure that you are in the best place that you can be. Be in control of your own life, be in control of your own development because all you need to do this is *YOU*! All the light and all the love is right there waiting to be utilised. They are the only tools that we need to do this job right. Then all else will surely follow just as night follows day.

Many twin flame aspects are coming together now, also for the task in hand. They are coming to shine their light and to share their love with the planet. The two of us are twin flames living an awakened life together, happy to talk about anything at all without the fear of ridicule or humiliation. We realise that this is a special position to be in. There would have been many lives when this wasn't necessarily the case, when we would have lived separate lives. But we have built up to this wonderful physical incarnation as a duo for this special time. However, this isn't the case for everyone. How many people are in a relationship where they are the only spiritually aware party, spiritual growth stifled by a partner who is simply not yet ready for a revelation of this magnitude? They long to be released from the chains of doubt, wanting to be lifted above that brick wall by the hand of someone who can carry the weight. How must they feel to be worried and concerned about sharing a wonderful experience with a loved one, just out of the love for that person and a desire to get them involved in something that's beyond our realm; to share in obvious delight? Ask yourself this... would you not want to share in something of this scale?

Everyone needs to express themselves, everyone needs to be able to spread their wings and fly to dizzy heights because we are limitless, we are all a massive soul bursting out from the seams of a physical body. We owe it to ourselves and also to the ones who look towards us to help them and answer their many questions, to allow self-growth from within. Otherwise we are confined to the views of the un-awakened, almost to keep the peace.

We often attend a number of mind body and spirit events and at many, we have spoken to people who have told us that we were the first to hear of their amazing spiritual and supernatural experiences. Experiences of being visited regularly by light beings; experiences of being able to psychically tap into the cosmic internet and pull information from it, experiences of realising that they were more than just human. Their fantastic stories had been untold until that point, hidden from friends, family and partners because of the ridicule they feared they would be subjected to. Every one of them needed to know that the events that they were experiencing day after day were actually normal, and they *are*. It is just another reality, it is a realm and level of consciousness different from our own, yet it is all connected by the oneness that is everything and everyone. None of them are alone in their experiences, however bizarre they may have seemed. You are never alone in what you know; we all know because we are all a part of everything else, a part of each other. If we hurt somebody, we are hurting ourselves, if we love somebody, we are loving ourselves.

We are all sparks of the same fire that created us. We are all a multi-dimensional existence on many levels, many facets of the same energy. When others, including family, don't want to engage in what we have to say, well they are simply not yet ready to embrace a greater truth, but they like us are 'a spiritual being having a human experience' too. Never go within and hide your beliefs, never pretend that they haven't happened when they clearly have, for that is the real you. Develop and expand the real you because that is your truth, that is who you really are so be proud of *you*. Be patient and understanding to those who run two steps behind, hold out your hand and ease them along gently until they are fast enough to run alongside.

The long lost city of Atlantis once existed and on some level, still does. This was a society where all were free and not afraid to shine their light and their love. A society where Angels, Masters and other Cosmic beings walked freely amongst the populous and were involved in everyday life; a place where society was joined together as one and love was the only rule. Technology was powered by crystals and all were self and spiritually aware. Gifts and abilities were developed and allowed to blossom and personal growth was encouraged. This subject wasn't taboo and at the height of its existence, Atlantis was a paradise.

Atlantis was a continent in the Atlantic Ocean between the British Isles and America up until around 14,000 years ago when it sank to the bottom of the sea to rest, lost to the ocean floor following the great fall. What was once a beautiful place became corrupted by the darkness that still influences world events even today and Atlantis disappeared out of sight and out of mind. Many of the leaders of Atlantis fled to various places such as Egypt, and formed smaller colonies in an attempt to recreate the beauty of their former home. Many stories have been written and told about Atlantis and many questions have been asked. It was, until its downfall, the ideal society. Illness was cured before it took hold by vibrational re-alignment and healing with crystals, and death was seen as an advancement of the soul. Atlanteans realised that all existence is energy and that if that energy flowed around the body with ease, then they were healthy, and if that energy became blocked in any way, then the energy would flow with dis-ease. The healthier your body is and the more energy flowing around it with ease, the more light that you can hold and shine. The opposite can be said if the energy is flowing with dis-ease due to any blockages, energetic and physical. This is another reason that our food, water, air and environment is littered with toxic chemicals today. It is an attempt to stop the life force energy from flowing with ease through our bodies, weakening our energy fields and therefore preventing the amount of cosmic light energy that we can hold.

Atlantis still has an influence today. Most people have heard of the Bermuda triangle, a place where mystical and mysterious things occur and objects such as planes and ships inexplicably disappear never to be seen or heard from again. It is thought that the Bermuda triangle phenomenon is simply the great crystal of Atlantis which was never deactivated when she sank to the ocean floor. The great clear quartz crystal was the powerhouse that fuelled all things on this wonderful continent and at certain times when the sun and moon shine at certain angles upon the ocean floor, it allegedly activates this great crystal. This in turn creates an energy vortex that turns everything that passes through into anti-matter and sometimes even transports people and objects to other dimensions from where they haven't yet found a way back. Hence the reason objects disappear but only at certain times when the crystal has been activated by these events in sequence. So sometimes people may pass without incident, and at other times, they vanish, depending on whether or not the crystal is activated at that particular moment.

Dolphins are the keepers of the ancient secrets of the continent of Atlantis and they will return that knowledge when the human race is ready and responsible enough to receive it. A good choice, as these creatures are so loving, intelligent and full of light. Dolphins came to Earth from Sirius, a constellation that is visible to the naked eye in the night sky. When the time comes, humanity will be telepathically able to receive such information and will be intelligent enough to be able to decipher it. Atlantis was once a thriving and peaceful, spiritual paradise that was unfortunately lost when man's ego began to take control. The light dimmed, so too did the love for each other. We have been in a quagmire ever since, but times are a changing!

With all that has been discussed so far, consider this; consider, that in everything they do, in all the pain they cause, the devastation they inflict upon us and the downright violation of our freewill and humanity, the fallen ones that choose to reside in the shadows, could actually be doing us a favour... Consider that at the heart of the matter, these dark souls actually love us so much that they volunteered to take on a role that they knew would teach us so much, make us so much stronger and increase our soul development tenfold. Consider that they may have been brave to do so, knowing that they would have to scar us so deep, that they could lose us forever, all in the name of *love...*

We all choose our roles according to our needs and the stage of development that we are at. The dark ones have gotten lost in their role. They have taken the show too far and now is the time to bring it back. They have a light under their shadowy armour too and at some point it will be exposed. Although they are currently blinded, blinded by their egos, their greed, their selfishness and self-importance, they will soon rediscover that we are all part of the same consciousness, albeit that they currently reside at the lower end of the spectrum. They have played their part and more and are now having to be dragged kicking and screaming from the helm like stubborn children. Their darkness has helped, and is helping us to measure how light we are.

We may all have played a dark role at some point in our incarnations, but to be where we are right now, with person after person waking up and breaking free of the illusion, we are well on our way to becoming en-lightened again. Everything that we have ever done has led us to this point. Let's use what we have learned wisely because now is the time.

"Do not let your fire go out, spark by irreplaceable spark. In the hopeless swamps of the not quite, the not yet, and the not at all, do not let the hero in your soul perish and leave only frustration for the life you deserved, but never have been able to reach. The world you desire can be won, it exists, it is real, it is possible, it is yours".

- Ayn Rand

The dark is a great teacher, but the lesson's over. There is a new class in town.

CHAPTER 13:

This Is It!

The people of the world are waking up, for sure. Unrest in nearly every country, protests against the systems of unfair rule, even police officers and army generals, who are still serving are joining the people, deciding not to side with government authority. Governments have to have a strong arm, which is usually the police and armed forces who help to maintain their power. Without this, they have no power. People are sick and tired of injustices and are growing in number to change the system. So when the very strong arm of the law rebels, someone, somewhere amongst the corridors of power, should be very worried. We have all been taken for a fool for far too long, now is the time for it to stop, and stop it will. Every part of our lives are controlled by our governments, they have no right to do this and we must take our power back. We are free spirits, birds without a cage, let's fly. Our leaders say that they are appointed by the people to serve the people, do you feel served? The only service I can see is self-service. Imagine if come election time, we all voted for not one party or the other... but none of them! What a message that would send from we the people; that we are not happy with this current charade of a system.

Sarah and I are passionate people who simply could not help or allow the governments to cling onto control. We could no longer go against our own integrity and manipulate crime figures and continually fail to assist people in need because the system was only interested in targets. Emergency response times altered to suit targets when all along the public suffered. No more could we be a part of this backwards often self-serving occupation and we left. When you have banged your head against the wall for long enough and haven't changed anything it is time to vote with your feet and leave and try a different angle. The time of moaning had passed and the time for action was upon us, and we took it.

It hits us deep to see so much control, injustice and unfairness in today's society, especially when you realise that it is manipulated to be that way. It is no accident that we have famine, war, and decimation of the populous, illnesses, taxation, and constant worry about money. It is no accident that those at the top control the world's finances because they measure their warped success on their material possessions and what they have over others. It is no accident that people are made to focus on everything other than their true self, this is exactly what keeps the control system going. Because most of us are oblivious we are kept under the thumb and as soon as we realise just what and who we are, we are no longer controlled. We have written this book to try and educate people as to what is going on around them and then we hope that more and more will take a stance and find out the true essence of what and who they truly are. It is our life's purpose to do these things. We would never encourage anyone to do anything that we would not do ourselves.

Sarah and I left a secure recession proof career at a time when people were being made redundant, not out of choice. It went against the tide and it raised a number of eye brows, when we decided to resign from the police force. It taught us about life, humanity, and the problems of our society but most of all it gave us the opportunity to serve and to do our best, within the confines of a system. For everyone who called us and needed us we did our best to be there to help them at their time of need. This was something that we took very seriously.

Although the uniform has long since gone, leaving only memories within the filing cabinets of our minds, our principles still remain. Our burning desire to assist and make a difference is as young, fresh, alive and vibrant as it was and ever possibly could be. And yes we miss it, we miss what it once was, not what it has become. Sarah and I now know much more as a result of this period in our lives, experiences we would not have had without it, for which we are very grateful. It is an extra strand of our DNA, it is a life purpose, it is a fire that cannot be unlit.

So what now for us? Where do we go from here? We go into the endless font of universal knowledge and then we resurface and we tell every single person, animal, and mammal, speck of dust and grain of sand that we come into contact with about the wonderment that exists around each and every one of us. You have the right to access what is yours and you deserve to be told of the magnificence that we all have as a natural gift from a place of pure love and affection.

We have learned a lot on this journey that we find ourselves on, that we find ourselves living with each and every second of each and every day and so on until infinity is reached, if indeed it can be reached. It never ends and with each answer comes yet another question.

We want you to realise that we are all brilliant; we all have such magnificent abilities. We are the pedestal that other beings wish to be upon. We have the opportunity to live a physical life, where others missed out. Our education and soul growth is advanced and whole as a result of us being upon planet Earth to learn and develop in times of such spiritual ascension. And most of all, not forgetting the support we all have during this task.

Let us find out the truth together like the human family we are, not segregated by continental boundaries, languages or colour. That is merely a red herring to divert our attention onto insignificant distractions, that will inevitably lead us astray and far away from the truth, as it is intended to do. Let us ignite a passion that replicates the passion that created us all those aeons ago, when we were a spark and ember of energetic life of the purest kind. Let us share in the infinite knowledge that we are all 'One' and let us be at peace with each other instead of terminating a fellow existence. Then and only then can we be worthy of the higher realms of purity and love.

Spiritual is a state of being. Awareness allows you to know at what stage your development is at. Everyone is already enlightened they just need to be aware that they are enlightened. That is where you have to work, not working to become what you already are. You need to work to realise that this is so. You cannot become what you already are, but you need to become aware of what you are. You don't need anyone else to give you what you already have within you. Don't give your power away to anyone else, empower yourself because all that you will ever need is within you already and it will be self-activated when the time is right for you. Take responsibility for yourselves and your own life. We are all amazing. It is your life and only you can live it.

It is said that the tide waits for no man. But if man waits for the tide, he will be ready because he knows it is coming. Prepare yourself for a new golden age and prepare yourself to do your part in this time of awakening. Let's lift our consciousness and rise above insignificant things together.

"You cannot solve a problem with the same level of consciousness that created it". - Albert Einstein

Now is the time to rise, now is our chance. This is our time!

"So here we are, on the brink,
A new dawn in our sights.
The time has come, it has begun,
Together, we'll reach new heights.
The enlightenment that we share,
Was always there,
And it can happen overnight.
Like slaves we've been for far too long,
Now it's time to sing our song.
From the murky depths of our pit,
Together we rise...

THIS IS IT"!

- Sarah Feeley

Best wishes to you all on your journeys of awareness and self-discovery.

In Love & Thanks,

Michael & Sarah Feeley

11:11